The Man God Uses

by

Oswald J. Smith

Rickfords Hill Publishing Ltd.

Published by
RICKFORDS HILL PUBLISHING LTD.
24 High Street, Winslow, Buckingham, MK18 3HF, UK.
www.rhpbooks.co.uk

First Published in 1932
This edition 2015

ISBN: 978-1-905044-46-7

Printed and bound in Great Britain
by CPI Group (UK) Ltd, Croydon CR0 4YY

Contents

1

The Man God Uses

Never will I forget that period in my life when I wanted, more than anything else, to be used of God. As I rode my mule through the beautiful ravines of the Kentucky hills, or paced back and forth in my little, lonely cabin among the mountaineers, I cried out to God in the agony of my soul, "Lord, use me. Make me a soul-winner. Send me out as an evangelist. Let me see revival. Don't let me settle down in an ordinary pastorate and accomplish nothing. I have only one life to live and I want to invest it for Thee. Let me live for others. Enable me to win lost men and women to the Lord Jesus Christ. Let Thy blessing rest upon my ministry."

Then I would pray like this: "Lord, what are the qualifications for evangelistic work? How may I be used by Thee? Are there conditions to be met? If so, reveal them to me. What must I do? Make known the prerequisites. Help me to meet the conditions whatever they may be so that I may not waste my life. I must not fail."

Then as I studied God's Word I found the qualifications, and I faced them, one by one, as God revealed them to me. There they were, clearly stated. These conditions I now want to pass on to you, for I believe that you, too, want to be used of God. You, too, realize that you have but one life to live and you do not want to waste it. You want it to count for souls. You want to know the qualifications for the work of evangelism and revival. Let me mention them one by one, just as God revealed them to me so long ago.

1. A vision of the utter bankruptcy of the human race

I think that is where we must begin. Until God gives us a vision of the utter bankruptcy of the human race, we will not get far with our evangelistic work. We must know that the race is bankrupt. We must realize that men are dead in trespasses and in sins, that there is no good thing in any man. We must know something of the utter depravity of the human heart.

As long as we think there is a spark of divine life in the heart of man, we will not accomplish much in our evangelistic work; for we will then conclude that all we have to do is to fan that spark into a flame and all will be well.

That, you see, rules out the new birth entirely. There is then no need of conversion, for if man already has life, he does not have to receive life. He has merely turned his back on his Father God and has wandered away. The work of the evangelist, then, is to persuade him to right about face, to turn back to God.

Such an idea implies that we are all children of God, which according to the Bible is untrue. Until we have been born again, we are children of Satan and we do not belong to the family of God at all. Only the new birth can make us children of God. No, my friend, there is no spark of divine life in any man; therefore there is nothing to fan into a flame. Men are dead, lost, undone, utterly depraved, with no hope of life apart from a new birth.

That is why I say that we must realize something of the utter bankruptcy of the human race. We must know that man who is dead must be quickened into life, that he is utterly hopeless in himself, and that only God can meet his need. That qualification is of paramount importance and no evangelist can be successful until he has it.

2. A realization of the adequacy of God's salvation

On the one side, there is the utter bankruptcy of the human race, but on the other, a salvation adequate to meet the need. In other words, God has a remedy. God has a cure. He has made adequate provision. God can quicken men from death into life. He has provided for the bankruptcy of the human race, for those who are dead in trespasses and in sins.

Over nineteen hundred years ago, through His only begotten Son, the Lord Jesus Christ, He made that provision. Hence, when you and I go out into our evangelistic work, realizing as we do that men are dead in trespasses and sins, that they are utterly helpless and hopeless in themselves, and that the human race is absolutely bankrupt, we know that we have a glorious Gospel, a wonderful Saviour, a marvellous provision—all that is needed to meet man's desperate plight.

There is no other such message. With joy in our hearts and assurance in our souls, we can go with the Gospel of the Lord Jesus Christ, knowing that it will work. The most desperate character, the man farthest away from God and deepest in sin, can be rescued through the power of the Gospel of Jesus Christ. That is why Paul exclaimed, "I am not ashamed of the gospel of Christ: for it is the power of

God unto salvation to every one that believeth..." (Rom. 1:16). The Gospel is the remedy. There is no other. You and I must realize that and never turn to anything else. This only must be our message. Any other cure will be inadequate. God's Gospel is man's only hope.

The United Nations do not have the solution to the problem. No statesman has the solution. No politician can meet the need. No government is adequate. You and I are the only ones who have the solution, and our solution is the Gospel. There is no other. "Christ died for our sins" (1 Cor. 15:3).

The Gospel solves all problems. The Gospel is effective when nothing else is. The Gospel meet all needs. Nothing else can. Therefore it is the Gospel that we must preach. Thank God, we can preach it with the utmost assurance.

Now, my friends, unless you believe that the Gospel is the solution and that there is no other, you will not get far in your evangelistic work. Unless you know that man in his helplessness and hopelessness is utterly bankrupt, and that apart from the Gospel he is beyond recovery, you will not accomplish much. Unless you really believe that man is utterly depraved, that he is dead in trespasses and in sins, and that you have the one and only remedy, the Gospel of the Lord Jesus Christ, and that this remedy can meet his direst need, hopeless though he may seem, you will have but little success as you seek to evangelize.

3. A life given over to one great purpose

You remember that the Apostle Paul said, "This one thing I do." Paul was a man of one thing. The man who is going to be successful in evangelistic and soul winning work is the man who has set everything else aside, who has become a man of one thing, one purpose, one aim in life. Any man with divided interests, any man with many schemes, plans and programmes, any man who is interested in other things, is not going to be successful as an evangelist. The one who is going to succeed is the one who has but one great purpose in his life.

When I was a student I never dreamed of getting married until I had graduated and had commenced my ministry. For a student to take upon him the responsibility of a wife and family is a tremendous financial burden. If his interests are thus divided, how can he concentrate on his studies and expect to succeed in his work? Would it not be better to wait until he is through with his schooling before taking such a step?

I never have been able to understand how some ministers can carry on their work as ministers and at the same time go into business on the side. If God calls a man to preach the Gospel, he should live by the Gospel. There is no reason why he should make a little money on the side. If he turns to business, he is going to become interested in business. He will give thought to it and he will not be a man of one thing. Part of his time will be spent in the ministry and part in business.

I have learned that the ministry demands all that there is of a man. It requires his entire attention, all his thought, all his study, both day and night. He must be completely wrapped up in his vocation. He must be given over absolutely to the one great work to which God has called him. If he is trying to make a little money on the side, if he is interested in business of one kind and another, he is not going to be able to concentrate on the one great work to which God has ordained him.

The monks had the right idea. They felt that they should withdraw from the world to lock themselves up in a monastery so as to devote their entire time to God. They felt that they should give up all other interests and have nothing more to do with the world so that they might serve God perfectly. I say, their aim was right, their purpose was right, although their method was wrong. God's plan is that we should mingle with our fellow men and yet be utterly devoted to Him.

Can a wife be a successful wife if she is interested in another man? Can a husband be a successful husband if he is interested in another woman? You know the answer. How then can any man called of God be a successful evangelist if he has other irons in the fire? It is simply impossible. The evangelist must be a man of one great purpose in life. He must be able to say with the Apostle Paul, "This one thing I do."

My friend, have you a number of different interests? Are you trying to do several things instead of devoting yourself to the one great work to which God has called you? Do you want to be a success? Are you anxious to win souls to the Lord Jesus Christ and to know something of the glory of revival? Then, I say again, concentrate on one thing. Give yourself wholly to God and to the work of evangelism.

Do you remember the words of the Apostle Paul: "No man that warreth entangleth himself with the affairs of this life; that he may please him who hath chosen him to be a soldier" (2 Tim. 2:4)? Timothy was to be a man of one thing. Paul made it clear to him that no man that allows himself to be entangled in worldly affairs could ever be a successful soldier. So it is with the evangelist. If he is going to serve God as God wants him to serve, he must free himself from every other interest.

You want God to use you? Well, then, are you willing to pay the price? Are you prepared to let everything else go and become a man of one thing? Will you devote your entire life to this one thing, to see to it that nothing else attracts you, that nothing else interests you, nothing else absorbs your attention? Are you prepared to concentrate, to give yourself wholly to God's service, to become a man of one great purpose in life? If you are, God will use you for His glory and honour, and your evangelism will be successful.

4. A life from which every hindrance has been removed

Do you remember that statement in Psalm 66:18: "If I regard iniquity in my heart, the Lord will not hear me"? He will not even bend down and listen to what I say, if I harbour, if I regard, iniquity sin in my heart. All sin must be put away.

My friend, this may be the reason that God is not using you. It may be that you have an idol in your life, that there is an Achan in the camp. Perhaps you are burdened by a weight of some kind, or a habit that you are unwilling to give up. You may not even recognize it as a sin, but it comes between you and God, and it makes it impossible for God to use you.

Day by day, you try to go forward, but something drags

you back, a weight of some kind holds you down and makes it impossible for you to run the race that God wants you to run. A habit, harmless in itself, is keeping God's power from your life; and because you will not forsake your sin, because you refuse to renounce it utterly, God is unable to use you.

Sin is bound to retard your progress. It grieves the Holy Spirit, and you will never know the blessing and power of God on your life and your ministry until you are ready to renounce it forever, to turn from it utterly and never to indulge in it again.

You will have to face that Achan in the camp, that idol in your heart, that habit in your life, whatever it may be. There must be a clean break. As long as you go on doing what you are now doing, God will withhold His power. His anointing you will never know, His blessing you cannot experience. If you want to succeed as an evangelist, if you want to see revival in your ministry, then break with sin.

Why not do it now while you are young? Why wait until it gets a hold on you, until it becomes a confirmed habit? Why not deal with it before the chains have wrapped themselves around you so tightly that it is next to impossible to break them? Now is the time to deal with sin. You have your whole life before you. If you want God to use you, then be definite, be emphatic.

This should be your prayer: "Search me, O God, and know my heart; try me, and know my thoughts: and see if there be any wicked way in me, and lead me in the way everlasting" (Ps. 139:23-34). It may be that with all your talents and your gifts, all your accomplishments, all your education, you will be a complete and miserable failure in your evangelistic work, simply because there is something in your life, something in your heart, that grieves the Spirit of God and makes it impossible for Jesus Christ to use you, as He wants to, for His honour and His glory. Let Him search you then. Let Him try you. Let Him reveal the Achan in your heart. Then confess it, put it away, and come clean with God, that He may bless and own your ministry.

5. A life placed absolutely at God's disposal

Thus far we have been dealing with the negative side. Now we come to the positive. God's great purpose is that our lives should be placed completely and absolutely at His disposal. That is why we have the statement again and again: "Yield yourselves unto God."

No potter can do anything whatever with clay that continually resists the potter's attempt to shape it. If the potter cannot make the kind of vessel he wants to make, the reason is that there is something in the clay that resists his touch. Just as soon as that hindrance has been removed and the clay yields itself absolutely to him, the potter can make any kind of vessel he desires to make. So it is with your life and mine. If God is going to use us for His honour and glory, if His power is going to rest upon us, if He is going to bless our evangelistic and soul-winning ministry, then our lives must be placed absolutely at His disposal.

As long as we have any will of our own, God can do little with us. His will must become our will, and as soon as His will does become our will, then He can begin to bless us. We should be able to say with the Lord Jesus, "I delight to do Thy will, O my God."

God never acts as a taskmaster. He never compels us to do something that we do not want to do. First of all He makes us willing, and then we delight in obeying Him. In other words, His will, as I have already stated, becomes our will and then there is only one will to obey. We have placed ourselves absolutely at God's disposal.

What could a doctor do for a patient as long as the patient refused his remedy? The patient must place himself absolutely in the hands of the doctor and must be perfectly willing to accept the prescription given him by the doctor. Only then is there any hope of recovery. As long as the patient goes his own way, takes his own medicine and refuses the prescriptions the doctor gives, little can be done for him. He must place himself in the hands of the doctor.

So it is with you and with me. Until we place ourselves absolutely at the disposal of God, God can do little for us. God wants your yielded life, and He will never be satisfied with you until, like a slave, a willing slave, you place yourself entirely at His disposal. Then He can use you for His glory.

6. A ministry of prevailing prayer

There is nothing more important than this. Jacob, you remember, wrestled with God in prayer. We do little wrestling today. We get up in the morning, fall down beside our bed, mumble off a few words of prayer and then hurry off to our work. Then at night, when we are weary, tired and exhausted, we do the same again, and climb into bed.

That, for the most part, is all that prayer means to us.

But that was not the way Jacob prayed. He wrestled all night. Some have never learned how to wrestle in prayer. Therefore they do not know how to prevail. Not until we prevail with God will we prevail with men, and to prevail with men we must learn how to travail.

Jesus knew what it was to travail in prayer. He spent, you remember, whole nights in prayer. Again and again His disciples found Him alone with God in some solitary place, pouring out His soul in agonizing prayer. You and I know but little of that kind of praying; but until we have learned how to get alone with God and travail in prayer, we will not be able to accomplish much. Not until then will He commence to use us, to answer our prayers and to glorify Himself in our ministry.

Charles G. Finney had such a burden of prayer. Time after time he went out into the woods, or to some solitary place, and there agonized in the presence of God. Sometimes he was unable even to put his petitions into words. He tells us that he could only groan and weep, so tremendous was the burden that rested upon him. No wonder God used him. No wonder he became the greatest revivalist of all time. No wonder God glorified Himself in his ministry. Finney knew how to agonize in prayer.

Every man used of God has been a man of prayer. If you have never learned how to pray, if you have never learned how to wrestle with God, if you have never learned how to agonize, if you know nothing about travail of soul, then you do not know what it means to get spiritual results. If you want to see God glorified in your ministry, you will have to become first and foremost a man of prayer.

7. A ministry saturated with the Word of God

I know ministers who never turn to the Word of God except to get sermons. Any man who does that will never get far in evangelistic work. You and I need to turn to the Word of God for the sake of our spiritual welfare. We ought to know the Book from cover to cover, and there is only one way to know it and that is to read it. Read it from Genesis to Revelation. Read it again and again. Meditate on it, mark it, study it, become saturated with it. Read it until it becomes a very part of you. Only then will God be able to use you as He wants to.

If you are not familiar with the weapon that you are going to use, you will find yourself at a disadvantage when you attempt to use it. Our weapon is the Word of God. Unless we are familiar with it, unless we know how to use it, we are not going to get far in our work of evangelism. God's Word must be both on our tongues and in our hearts. We must know it and meditate on it until it becomes a part of us. As we lie awake at night let us quote it again and again until we are saturated with it.

It is not our word, remember, that God uses; it is His Word. What we say may accomplish a little. What God says will accomplish much. Let us, then, use the Word, and in using it, know it. Therefore, again I say, let us read it until it becomes a part of us. There is no substitute for a knowledge of the Word.

8. A ministry with a vital message for a lost world

Why are you going to the foreign field? Why do you want to become a missionary? What do you expect to do "out there"? What have you for the heathen? Are you going to take them social service, or education? Is it your plan to raise their standard of living? Are you going to the foreign field to give them a little of our Western civilization? Is it your thought to concentrate on hospital and medical work?

My friend, if you are going to the foreign field for any of these reasons, then I would advise you to stay at home. There is no place for you in the regions beyond. Leave all non-evangelistic work to the United Nations. They can do a much better job than you can. They have more money, skilled workers and resources than will ever be yours. They have the equipment that is needed. They can educate the heathen. They can carry on medical work. They can take care of social services. They can impart Western civilization and culture. These are the by-products of Christianity. The main work of the missionary is to preach the Gospel.

Unless you are going out with but one message, you ought not to go. Your message should be John 3:16: "For God so loved the world, that He gave His only begotten Son, that whosoever believeth in Him should not perish, but have everlasting life." Unless you are going with that message, the message of God's salvation for a lost and perishing world, unless you are going to proclaim eternal life to those in heathen darkness, you had better stay at home.

Why are you going into the ministry? What is your purpose in preaching the Gospel of the Lord Jesus Christ? Do you want to entertain? Are you entering the ministry for the sake of a living? Are you interested in the money you can make? Are you doing it because it is the respectable thing to do and because it will give you prestige and influence? Is that your purpose?

Then, my friend, I say to you also, you had better seek another position. You had better look for something else, because God's blessing will never rest upon you, if these are your reasons. Unless you are going into the ministry with the message of God's salvation, unless you are going to present to those in sin and darkness a living Saviour and proclaim the message that "Christ died for our sins," unless you are going to say to the lost and perishing, "Behold the Lamb of God that taketh away the sin of the world," again I say, you had better turn to something else. The ministry is no place for you. It isn't worthwhile.

I am now thinking of a man in London, England. He visited two churches. In the morning he went to the City Temple, there in the heart of the great metropolis. He listened to one of the most eloquent sermons to which he had ever listened, and as he came out he was heard to exclaim, "What a wonderful sermon." At night, he went to Spurgeon's Tabernacle, that world famous pulpit, that great auditorium with its two huge galleries made famous by Charles H. Spurgeon, the prince of preachers, and as he came out he was heard to exclaim, "What a wonderful Christ!"

If your purpose is to preach great sermons, then you had better give up. The world does not need sermons, it needs a message, and there is all the difference in the world between a sermon and a message. You can go to a seminary and learn how to preach sermons, but you will have to go to God to get messages. Sermons will never influence your congregation but messages will. Sermons appeal to the intellect, messages to the heart. What people need to-day are not great sermons but great messages. We must go out to present Christ, the living Saviour.

The world, I say, is waiting for God's messengers. If you are going into the pulpit to present Christ, a living Christ for a dying world, then God will bless you and use you for His glory. You will be engaged in the greatest of all vocations, that of the ministry, and you will never re-gret having responded to the call of God. At the end of life you will look back over your ministry and thank God for a life spent in the service of the Lord Jesus Christ.

9. A ministry in the anointing of the Holy Spirit

There are those today who are almost afraid to talk about the Holy Spirit. There has been so much cold conservatism and so much fanaticism regarding the Holy Spirit that they scarcely mention Him. Yet He is the third Person of the Trinity, the Executor of the Godhead, the One who takes the leading place in the Book of Acts. It was the Holy Spirit who actually did the work. He it was who guided and directed the apostles. He it was who led. The Holy Spirit convicted of sin and started revivals. He—God, the Holy Ghost—was the One who founded the Early Church.

Today, to a large extent, He is ignored. We have an idea that we can get along without Him, that education and training will take His place and somehow become a substitute for His power, and we have endeavoured to carry on our ministry in the energy of the flesh, apart from the Holy Spirit altogether. It is high time, I say, that we gave Him His rightful place, for He is the One who must do the work. Unless you and I know something about the anointing of the Spirit of God, we will not get far in the service of God.

Down through the years of my ministry I have studied the lives of those whom God has used, and I have discovered that: every one was an anointed man. Each, evangelist or revivalist, knew something of a crisis experience in his life, when the Holy Ghost took over and began using him.

Evan Roberts knew that anointing. I will never forget the day I called on him, when I was in Wales. He was not home, but I saw the house in which he lived, and I felt that even the ground on which I stood was holy. Later, he wrote me a letter, in his own handwriting, and a few months after, passed on to be with his Lord. Evan Roberts, I say, knew the anointing of the Holy Spirit. Charles G. Finney knew that anointing. He knew what it was to be endued with power from on high. D. L. Moody knew it. John Wesley knew it. Every man whom God has used, all down through the centuries, has known what it means to be anointed by the Spirit of God.

Anointed men are not satisfied with education and training. They know that something more is needed and that God cannot use them until they have experienced the anointing. So they wait in the presence of God until they have been endued with power from on high. Then they go out and accomplish more in a few weeks or months in the demonstration and power of the Spirit than they could have accomplished in the energy of the flesh in years.

God wants anointed men today, and unless you and I know something of the anointing, we will not get far in the work of evangelism. So important have I considered it that I wrote a book on it, *The Enduement of Power*.

You do not have to go into fanaticism. There is a middle of the road experience, a Scriptural position that you can take, an experience set forth in the Word of God and recognized by men of God all down the centuries, an experience that may be yours. If you want to amount to anything in the service of God, you will see to it that it is yours and that you, too, are an anointed man.

I do not care whether you go to the foreign field, or whether you work among the heathen here at home, whether you do missionary work abroad, or whether you hold evangelistic campaigns in your own country, you must know the anointing of the Holy Spirit. Otherwise, there will be a lack of power in your ministry and you will accomplish little. If you want to see God use you, if you want souls to be convicted and saved under your ministry, you will tarry until you have been endued with power from on high. You will become an anointed man.

10. A ministry characterized by the expectancy of faith

One time Charles H. Spurgeon sent his students out to hold open-air meetings on the streets of London. Day after day they came back to report. Some were successful, others were not. One day a young man with few gifts or talents approached Mr. Spurgeon with a downcast expression on his face. "Mr. Spurgeon," he said, "I cannot understand why it is I am not able to win souls to the Lord Jesus Christ. I am taking part in these open-air meetings, I have faithfully preached the Gospel and I am doing my dead level best, but there seems to be little or no response to my appeals." Spurgeon looked at the young man for a few moments and then he said this: "Do you mean to tell me that you expect God Almighty to save souls every time you preach?" The young man was taken aback. "Why no," he said, "I guess not. Of course not. I could hardly expect that. I haven't completed my training yet, and I haven't as many gifts and talents as others. No, I see, I am wrong, I shouldn't expect it." "Then," Mr. Spurgeon exclaimed, "that is why you do not see results." The young man did not have the expectancy of faith, and God's Word is, "According to your faith, be it unto you." If you do not expect results, you will not get them.

My friend, if you do not expect to see results, you will not see them. I quote again, "According to your faith, be it unto you." You are to step into the pulpit to preach the Gospel with the expectancy of faith. You ought to be just as certain of results when you commence to preach as you are when you actually see men and women walking down the aisles to accept Jesus Christ as Saviour.

All through the years of my ministry, I have extended the invitation. I cannot understand how any minister can be satisfied to preach the Gospel, pronounce the benediction and then go home without having seen anything happen. It seems to me that after I have spread the food on the table, I ought to give the people a chance to come forward and partake of it, and if I do not, I am leaving something vital out of my ministry.

Sunday after Sunday I have invited lost men and women as well as backsliders to come forward and accept Christ, and I can hardly remember a Sunday night through all the years of my ministry when I have not seen results. Night after night, I have seen them walk down the aisles, stand at the front and then go with the personal workers into the inquiry rooms, there to be dealt with individually. I am surprised when nothing happens. If I were to preach a gospel message, give an invitation and see no one respond, I would be amazed. I expect to see results.

I do not mean to say that all those who have come have been saved, but I have reason to believe that some at least have found Jesus Christ and are now God's children. When I step into the pulpit God seems to give me that expectancy of faith of which I have been speaking, so that I know perfectly well that when I have concluded my message and extended the invitation, there will be those who will respond. I think I would get out of the ministry if I could not see results.

Does not a lawyer expect a verdict? He does not speak to entertain. He talks to the jury in order to get a conviction; and unless he secures a verdict, his appeal has failed. So, too, should it be with the gospel preacher, with the evangelist. He should expect a verdict. He should get results. If he doesn't, there is something wrong. His ministry, I say, should be characterized by the expectancy of faith.

11. A ministry wholly devoted to the glory of God

My friend, if you are carrying on your ministry for any other purpose than the glory of God, it will not amount to much. If you are an evangelist for what you can get out of it, if you are preaching to exalt self, if you want an easy living, if you are after money or fame, you may see something of outward success, but you will never know the blessing of God. If you have any other motive save the glory of God, you cannot expect the kind of results that God wants to give. Your ministry must be for God's glory.

If that is not your purpose, then if I were you, I would get down before God and humble myself until all of self had been eliminated. I would ask God to break me so that I might glorify Him. For unless you put the glory of God first, you will be a dismal failure. You will never accomplish anything really worth while. If you are out to please yourself, God will not honour your ministry. You must be broken if He is to use you. Otherwise, sooner or later, there will be disaster.

I have tried to bring you face to face with the eleven qualifications that God has revealed to me. May I suggest that you go back over them, one by one, and then ask God to search your heart. I am sure that you want Him to use you, that you want to be a successful evangelist, and that you long for revival. Then face the prerequisites as I have outlined them and let God speak to you. He wants to use you. He longs to bless your ministry. But if there are hindrances in the way, He cannot; and it is for you to remove them, that is, if you want to be the Man God Uses.

2

The Separated Life

It is doubtful if there ever was a time when the note of Separation needed to be sounded more than today. The world has become so churchy and the Church so worldly that it is hard to distinguish the one from the other. The line of demarcation has been so completely broken down that churches, where revivals once flourished, whose spiritual life was at one time deep and strong, are today mere social centres over which God has long ago written the word "Ichabod"—"The glory has departed."

People seem to have the idea that we must mingle with the world and become like it in order to win souls and influence lives for God. Yet when a man falls into a deep well no one ever dreams of jumping down alongside of him in order to get him out. Instead he stays away up at the top and from there lets down a ladder or rope and thus lifts him up.

Ah, no! The men who have won souls and influenced other lives for God have been the men who have walked with God far above the masses, and thus from an altitude of spirituality have drawn others up to their level. The only way to win others is to be different ourselves and thus attract by something they lack, and by prevailing with God prevail with men.

Had Abraham gone to live with Lot in Sodom his influence would have availed but little. It was when he separated himself and stood afar off on the highlands of faith with God that his intercessions secured Lot's deliverance. Let us be separate. We must dwell apart with God.

Then I want to say that the world expects the Christian to be different. It has its own standard of what a saint should be. And even when it succeeds in drawing us down to its level it but mocks and laughs at our plight. No longer does it respect us nor reverence our position. We are then no better than others.

A young woman who saw no harm in dancing decided to do some personal work during the dance, and while gliding over the floor with her companion, she suddenly turned and asked him if he was a Christian.

"A Christian! No! Why, are you?" he exclaimed in amazement.

"Yes," replied the young woman. "I'm a Christian."

"Well, then, why are you here?" was the unexpected response.

Ah yes, the world expects the Christian to be different. Otherwise how will anyone know which is which? If there is no line of demarcation how will people know which side we are on? If we dress and act like the world how can anyone tell whether we are Christians or not? There must be a difference.

Now, separation has always been God's standard. Abraham had to leave his country, and his father's home, and in complete separation go he knew not whither. Moses refused to be called the son of Pharaoh's daughter, choosing rather to suffer affliction with the people of God than to enjoy the pleasures of sin for a season; esteeming the reproach of God greater riches than the treasures in Egypt. So also with the Israelites. They were a peculiar people, entirely separated from the nations around about them, representing God. In Ezra 9 and 10 and Nehemiah 13, when the line of separation had been broken down by mixed marriages there was no leniency shown. Heathen wives must be put away and separation of the severest character again instituted.

Yes, and separation is still the call of God. "Come out from among them, and be ye separate, saith the Lord," and, "Be ye not unequally yoked together with unbelievers" (2 Cor. 6:14-18). The world must be forsaken and separation maintained.

Let us remember our character. According to God's Word we are "pilgrims and strangers," "sojourners," a heavenly people in a foreign country. This is not our home.

I'm but a pilgrim here,
A stranger from afar;
And to my distant home
With many a battle scar,
My Lord will bear me safe at last
When pilgrim days on earth are past.

Enmity and hatred is the attitude of the world toward the true child of God. "If ye were of the world, the world would love his own: but because ye are not of the world, therefore the world hateth you" (John 15:19). What about it? Does the world hate you? If you are not of it, if you do not belong to it, and if you make it clear that you are a pilgrim and a stranger, then you will very quickly discover that the world hates you. You see it depends on the attitude you take toward it.

Now, the evidence of the separated life lies in the attitude of the heart, not the actions, towards the world. "Love not the world, neither the things that are in the world. If any man love the world, the love of the Father is not in him" (1 John 2:15). Hence, it is not necessary actually to take part in the things of the world. The real question is: Do you want to? Is there a desire? Does the world appeal and allure? If so, then there is no heart separation after all.

Listen again: "Ye adulterers and adulteresses, know ye not that the friendship of the world is enmity with God? Whosoever therefore will be a friend of the world is the enemy of God" (Jas. 4:4). Pretty plain language! Talk about a "worldly Christian"! God declares that the world's friend is His enemy. The one who loves the world does not love God. What then is my heart attitude? That is the important question, Do I love the world or do I love God? Am I the world's friend or God's friend? Would the word "adulterer" or "adulteress" be applicable to me? What is the real attitude of my heart toward the world? Not my actions but my thoughts, my likes and dislikes.

Now, the separated life means separation from:

1. *Worldly Pleasures.*

That was the choice Moses made when he repudiated the pleasures of sin (Heb. 11:24-26). The dance, the theatre, and the card party are not of God, but of the world. They were introduced not by spiritual leaders and saintly men, but by men of the world. The spirit of the world pervades such pleasures, and prayer and testimony in the midst of these things is out of the question. The two simply don't go together. The people who throng such gatherings do not attend nor take part in prayer meetings, nor are they interested in the spiritual work of the Church. Hence, the time must come when the true Christian is willing to obey the clear and emphatic command: "Come out from among them, and be ye separate," and to sing from the heart:

Goodbye, Old World, goodbye!
I want no more of thee,
For God is dearer far than thou canst ever be;
My soul is satisfied
With Christ the Crucified;
And all I need I find in Him alone.

2. Worldly Alliances.

"Be ye not unequally yoked together with unbelievers." No words could be clearer, no command more emphatic. God cannot honour the unequal yoke.

(1) Business Alliances.

The Christian who enters into partnership with an unbeliever or even with a so called worldly Christian is running a dangerous risk. Pray as he will he has no promise of blessing in God's Word. No wonder so many business enterprises fail. To disobey the plain Word of Scripture is to invite disaster. How can God bless what he has condemned?

(2) Lodge Alliances.

The lodge may be good enough for the man of the world, but for God's child the Church of Jesus Christ should more than suffice.

In the secret societies are to be found Unitarians, men who deny the deity of Jesus Christ. Even the name of the Lord Jesus is not permitted for fear of giving offence. And I want to say that the place that is not good enough for my Lord is not good enough for me. Nor could I go in when He is kept out.

Oh, how clearly God has spoken! "Be ye not unequally yoked together with unbelievers." Are Unitarians unbelievers? Most certainly. Then, thus saith the Lord: "Come out from among them, and be ye separate." God help us to obey.

But you say, "Once a Mason, always a Mason." Oh no! Not a bit of it. That is a man made law, and it has never been sanctioned by God. No, my brother, you can cut clean, renounce the whole thing, break every vow you ever took before your eyes were open, and step out into the clear light of God's Word.

(3) Marriage Alliances.

Oh, how many have admitted that the secret of all their unhappiness in married life lay in the fact that they disobeyed God and took on the unequal yoke. God's Word here also is very, very plain. "She is at liberty to be married to whom she will; only in the Lord" (1 Cor. 7:39). "Only in the Lord." And to marry one who is not in the Lord is to court disappointment. How can God's blessing rest on the home when His Word has been violated?

Many a young woman has had to face this problem and break her engagement; whilst others who have persisted in disobeying have lived to regret it beyond words to express. Nor does the plea that it is her purpose to marry, in order to win, avail in the least. The girl who fails to win her future husband for Christ before marriage has but little hope of winning him after.

Oh, Christian worker, don't, don't for your own sake, disobey the Word of God and enter the unequal yoke! It may seem hard now, but be certain of this: God has another and a far better plan for your life. To ignore His Word is dangerous. To obey it is always safe. There need be no question as to the results. Therefore, "Be ye not unequally yoked together with unbelievers."

3. *Worldly Companions.*

Here again there must be a breaking away. Worldly companions will not enjoy the Christians' prayer meeting, nor can the child of God take pleasure in their pursuits. Sooner or later the spirit of their association will dull spiritually unless a complete separation takes place. It is difficult to play with fire and not be burned.

But you say: How can I give them up? Child of God, you will not have to give them up. You live a spiritual life and they will very soon give you up. They will be as uncomfortable in your presence as you will be when with them.

Make friends of God's children. And whether they be brown or yellow, black or white, you will find them far more precious and the association closer and more binding than even that of blood relations out of Christ. They will understand when the members of your own family do not. And then, too, such friendships can never be broken. Death does not separate. Make friends, therefore, of those with whom you can associate not only here but throughout Eternity.

The Secret

Now, the secret of the separated life lies in "the expulsive power of a new affection." I will never forget the day Grace Armstrong was converted. It was at a Sunday afternoon meeting in Chicago. She just slid down on her knees and sobbed as though her heart would break. No one could console her. Then as she went out her girl friends told her that it would soon pass away.

"No, girls," responded Grace, "this never will pass away." And when young men telephoned her and invited her to the theatre, without a moment's hesitation she answered, "No." Old things had passed away in a single moment. No longer did she love the pleasures of the world. All things had become new. Christ was now in her heart and she had a new affection. She loved the prayer meeting, loved to stand and sing for her Saviour on the street corner, loved to do personal work, loved above everything else the House of God. There were no battles, no questions to answer, no problems to solve. When Christ came in in His glorious fullness the world went out. There was no room for it. Grace is now with her Lord, but oh, what a wonderful testimony she left before she went Home!

When I was a missionary among the Indians near Alaska, I lived for some time on what we called "hardtack." "Dog biscuit" I suppose would be the name in civilization. Now, it was hard, so hard that only by warming it could I manage to penetrate it with my teeth. Nevertheless I thoroughly enjoyed and relished it.

But there came a day when I returned to civilization, and began to eat bread and butter once more. And, what do you think? Why, I have never wanted hardtack since.

Not once have I pined for the old days and cried, "Oh, for a bit of hardtack once more!" And why? Simply because I've found something better.

Well, you can have the hardtack if you want it; but as for me, I am going to feast on bread and butter. I want the best. And, thank God, when we enter into the spiritual experiences of the New Birth and the Holy Ghost, we are fully satisfied; nor do we crave any more for the things of the world. Thus separation becomes easy. It is not hard to deny yourself something that you do not want. Thus, it is "the expulsive power of a new affection."

Since mine eyes were fixed on Jesus
I've lost sight of all beside,
So enchained my spirit's vision
Looking at the Crucified.

3

The Supreme Test

The early dawn was gently stealing over the hills far away in the distance, ushering in a new day and chasing away the darkness of the night. Save for the rumbling of the waves along the shore, and the occasional cry of some lonely sea bird, no sound broke the quiet stillness of the early morn.

"Lovest thou Me?"

The question was startling. The little group, sitting round the fire on the shore of the Galilean sea, glanced quickly up at the Speaker's face. With expectation gleaming in His eyes, He sat quietly gazing at but one, and waiting for the answer.

All through the long dreary night they had toiled with their nets and taken nothing. Then as the dawn began to break, a figure, strange, mysterious, stood upon the shore. Discouragement and weariness gave way to fear. With straining eyes they sought to pierce the rising mist, but all in vain, till, suddenly, the youngest of them recognized the silent, ghost-like form and cried:

"It is the Lord!"

Like a flash, Peter—poor, remorseful Peter, his great heart yearning with an almost superhuman devotion—leaps into the water, and with strong powerful strokes, soon reaches the shore. The others follow. The net is drawn in. A fire of coals is burning, and fish are cooking. Not a word is spoken until the Master, Himself, gives the simple invitation:

"Come and dine."

Quietly the food is eaten. All is still. Awe and reverence makes speech impossible. Finally, Jesus again breaks the silence with the words of our text:

"Lovest thou Me?"

It is Peter to whom He is speaking, great, blundering Peter; the disciple who so recently denied Him, who "went out and wept bitterly." He would test him. Peter must make a triple confession of his devotion for his threefold denial. He would try him by the highest possible standard, the "Supreme Test."

"Simon, son of Jonas, esteemest thou Me?"

He is pleading for that higher love, the love of the intellect or will, rather than the human emotion. But Peter is no longer sure of himself. He failed once; he may fail again. And so, unwilling to make the highest profession implied in his Master's question, he uses the word expressing mere emotional love or personal attachment:

"Yea, Lord, Thou knowest that I love Thee."

Again, the question is asked. The response is the same. Then the Master accepts Peter's own word, seeing that Peter will not rise to His, and for the third time asks:

"Simon, son of Jonas, lovest thou Me?"

And Peter, great noble Peter, his heart almost bursting with grief to think that his Lord should doubt him, replies with throbbing pulse and quivering voice:

"Lord, Thou knowest all things, Thou knowest that I love Thee!"

"Dost thou love Me?" With emotion
Comes the answer of devotion:
"Lord, Thou knowest that I love Thee."
"Feed My sheep," He answers, softly.

And we have called this question the "Supreme Test." But was it after all the highest test of devotion and loyalty, the most binding avowal that human lips could utter? Was there not a greater? Did Jesus make a mistake? The life of Peter does not seem to indicate any such mistake. Jesus didn't seem to think so. In fact, He was willing to base all on that one simple question. He knew what He was doing, knew that He was asking the most vital question in all language. And today, after the lapse of more than nineteen centuries, we may still look upon this question as the Supreme Test of our spiritual life.

First, The Supreme Test of Discipleship

Day by day, all down the centuries, Jesus Christ has been binding men and women to Himself. Not by force, not by fear, but by love. Satan was quite willing that He should have the kingdoms of the world provided He recognize His allegiance to him. But Jesus knew that it was not the Father's will to force men to obey Him. Ah, no! He would draw, not compel, win, not drive; men should choose Him of their own accord; they should be won by love. Such a union would be far closer, far stronger, and more lasting than forced obedience could ever be. Love had brought Him to earth; love had caused Him to die for a lost race, and love would draw men and women to Him. Could any oath of allegiance be stronger than the simple test He chose to put, "Lovest thou Me?"

Not a word does He ask regarding any one of a hundred questions that would naturally arise in the mind. Doctrine, dogma, creed, theology—not a word. Sin, repentance, service—not a syllable. One question only is asked. And mark you, it is His last chance. He is soon to leave. This is the best opportunity He would have for parting instructions and warnings. Has He no other word; are there no further conditions of discipleship; is there no creed or church formula to accept? No, none. And why? Because "Lovest thou Me?" includes and embraces all. The others will follow in their own places. The primary question will suffice for all else. "Lovest thou Me?" will lead on to all that is needful.

Thousands, today, are active church members, splendid workers, but they have no personal love for Jesus Christ. Form and ceremony can never suffice. To be true to the great fundamentals of the Faith does not prove that you are true in heart to Jesus. Multitudes who are right in their heads are wrong in their hearts. Brethren, I would rather be right in heart and wrong in head than right in head and wrong in heart. It is because of this that there is so much controversy and hard feeling today. God gave us a sickle, not to use on our brethren, but to gather sheaves. It is even possible to be a martyr for the Faith and yet not love Jesus Christ. Paul must have foreseen this when he wrote: "Though I give my body to be burned, and have not love, it profiteth me nothing."

Second, The Supreme Test of Conduct

No longer do we find it necessary to ask the old question regarding our attitude toward worldly things: "Is it wrong to do this?" "Is it a sin to do that?" We simply apply the "Supreme Test" to all our actions. It becomes "the expulsive power of a new affection." It is not a case of whether it is right or wrong to indulge in questionable amusements. A man becomes so filled with the Spirit of God, so permeated with the love of Christ, and so anxious to serve and please the One who has won his heart's affections, that there is no room for sin, no room for the world, and he will have absolutely no desire for the things in which the unsaved delight. Think you a man would injure one whom he really loved? Nay, verily! Hence, the one great question, the "Supreme Test" of all, is love.

Oh, my brother, tell me, do you love Him, do you love Him? If so, you will want to please Him. If so, you will want to follow Him. If so, you will be fully satisfied with Him, Him and Him alone. The world will no longer draw. Its charms will cease to exist so far as you are concerned, and you will no more crave its empty pleasures. Jesus, Jesus, Himself, will be your all and in all. You will feed upon Him, dwell with Him, abide in Him, love Him, and crown Him as King of your heart. All your questions will be easily settled if you really love Him.

> *Thou, O Christ, art all I want;*
> *More than all in Thee I find.*

Third, The Supreme Test of Service

In other words, it is the incentive of "love" rather than that of "duty." The follower of the Lord Jesus Christ serves his Master because he loves Him, and not because of any obligation he may wish to discharge.

What was it that drove David Brainerd to the savage

Indians of the great, howling wilderness? What was it that made him leave his home at twenty four years of age, and dwell alone in the heart of the wild, trackless forests of the interior; that enabled him though dying with consumption, weak and feeble from lack of food, long tiring rides on horseback, dismal, comfortless nights in the open woods under a pouring rain, to still press on month after month in order to tell his beloved Indians that God loved them, loved them to the extent that He gave His Son, His only Son, to die for them? What, I ask? Duty? Away with such a thought! No man would feel it his duty to do so much. No! No! It was "love." David Brainerd loved his Lord, and wanted to show it.

So with Judson, Livingstone, Morrison, Taylor, Carey, and all the great, heroic missionaries of the past. Yes, my brethren, and even so will it be with you, if you really love Him. You will prove it by glad, happy service. You will even lay down your life if need be—that is, if you love Him. Do you?

Oh, the breadth and length, the height and depth of His own great heart of infinite love and compassion! Love demands love. And nothing will satisfy a heart that loves except love. And so, because He Himself loves so greatly, He can be satisfied with nothing less than the love of His followers. What are wealth, houses, lands, luxury, and all that money can bestow to one who yearns for love? Love; and love only, is the ground of acceptance with Christ. Hence, "Lovest thou Me?" becomes the "Supreme Test" for every Christian.

In one of the larger cities of France where Mrs. Booth Clibborn had been holding evangelistic meetings, she was one day visited by the wife of a very wealthy Frenchman.

In her hand she held a small bottle marked "poison." In her heart was the calm determination to take her own life. She was only one of the hundreds of that sad and Godless country who go down to a suicide's grave. Before committing the deed, however, she made up her mind to see the only one in all France whom she felt she could trust, and look upon her face as she passed away. Let her own words tell the story:

"It was just the other day that I complained to my husband. Surprised and irritated, he replied:

"'Why, whatever do you want? You have my pocket book; you have my home; you eat at my table. All that wealth and position can give are yours, and yet you complain.'

"'I want your heart,' I replied, 'I want you to love me.'

"'Oh!' he exclaimed. 'You can't have that. That belongs to another. You may have everything else, but my heart, my love that is impossible.'"

And we may offer Jesus Christ everything else that we have, and still He will be unsatisfied. Love demands love. Nothing less can be sufficient. And now in the same tender, pleading tones, and the same yearning heart, He comes to you and to me, and once again we hear Him ask the question that constitutes the "Supreme Test," and demands an answer, "Lovest thou Me?"

If Jesus Christ should appear in our midst just now and personally put this question, "Lovest thou me?" to each one of us individually, what would we say? How would we answer Him? How searching it would be. Would we endeavour to avoid Him? Or are we in love with Jesus Christ? "We love Him," declared John. Do you? Do I?

4

What Does God Think of Me?

We are going to let God search us. We want to find out if possible just what He thinks of us. Our prayer will be the cry of the Psalmist, "Search me, O God, and know my heart; try me and know my thoughts; and see if there be any wicked way in me." And may He turn the searchlight of His Holy Spirit upon us until we are enabled to see ourselves as He sees us.

We are not trying to find out what the world thinks of us. Newspapers, books, and gossip may give the very opposite report of us to what God would give. They may praise while He condemns, or they may condemn where He praises. We are not even asking the opinion of our nearest and dearest friends. Even they may be deceived in us. "Man looketh on the outward appearance but God looketh on the heart." Our only desire is to discover what God thinks of us.

We shall some day stand face to face with God. And then, in the sight of the whole universe, we shall be unveiled and the innermost secrets of our hearts laid bare. The cloak that hid us from man will not hide us from God. Is it not better to find out now what He thinks of us, and if, as He weighs us in the balance we are found wanting, make up at once what we lack and get right with Him?

And so I ask, "What does God think of me?" God who searcheth the heart, as He looks into mine, what does He find there? Am I well pleasing in His sight? What does He think of me?

1. *What Does God Think of My Work?*

Does He find me genuine and sincere, free from all deception, and a stranger to hypocrisy? Never mind how much I blunder. The question is, Am I earnest? Am I sincere? If my motives are right, He will overlook my mistakes. Am I loyal to Him? Do I work from my heart, or are my labours merely professional? Is there any thought of personal gain?

Is my work counting for God? Does my life tell for Jesus? Am I able to lead others into a life of power and victory? Can I win souls to Christ? Do I ever try? Have I spoken to any one about his soul during the past year? Have I a message, or is my experience too shallow to mean anything to others?

2. *What Does God Think of My Social Relationships?*

Have I obeyed His summons, "Come out from among them, and be ye separate," and, "Be ye not unequally yoked together with unbelievers"? Are the things I am doing pleasing to Him? Can He smile upon me? Is there any pleasure that is driving Him from my heart and shutting out His presence? Is my conscience at rest, or does it trouble me when I do certain things and go to certain places? Am I willing to give up all for Jesus and to choose Him before the world? He gave up all for me. Do I want to please Him or am I going to argue the question with Him? Do I waste time that rightly belongs to Him?

3. *What Does God Think of My Devotional Life?*

Do I spend enough time with Him in private? Or am I hurried? Do I get alone with God? Do I love to meet Him in the inner chamber? Is communion with Him sweet to me? Is Jesus real? Does He fully satisfy?

Am I a student of God's Word? Do I study it in private, or is it all done in public? Does He unfold its secrets and make it real to me? Do I claim His promises and make them mine?

Is my life saturated with prayer? Do I pray and get answers? Have I learned how to pray? Do I merely say prayers, or do I pray? Are my prayers availing? Is prayer a real, vital thing to me?

4. *What Does God Think of My Christian Progress?*

Am I making progress in Spiritual things? Am I a growing Christian? Am I better this year than last? Is Jesus more real to me? Can my friends see any difference in me? Are the old weaknesses and failings of the flesh disappearing, and is the fruit of the Spirit becoming increasingly mine?"

Am I making progress against sin, especially my besetting sin? Has it been conquered, the sin that at one time conquered me? Do I want to be delivered from it? Is there still some cherished idol shutting out His peace and power, His presence, sunshine and love?

We often testify that Jesus satisfies. But suppose we turn it around and ask, "Is He satisfied?" For all that is important is our Lord's estimate of us. Has He been disappointed, or are we pleasing in His sight? *What does God think of me?*

5

The Sanctified Life

It is not my purpose to go into the doctrinal side of Sanctification, for I have learned that it is possible to know an experience doctrinally and yet fail to appropriate it in a practical way. Therefore I am going to be very simple and emphasize the experimental side of a sanctified life.

And first of all, I want to tell you three things that Sanctification is not, in order that you may the easier comprehend what it is.

What it is Not.

First, it is not freedom from temptation. The probability is that you will be tempted more as you live the sanctified life than ever before. Until then you have not been very dangerous to the kingdom of Satan; consequently he has not bothered much with you. But the moment you enter this experience he will do everything in his power to defeat you. Hence, Sanctification by no means ensures freedom from temptation.

Second, it is not a guarantee of safety from the possibility of sin. "Let him that thinketh he standeth take heed lest he fall." There is no condition in this life where a Christian is safe from the possibility of sin. Those who rise highest can fall lowest. Beware, then, of a false security, for Sanctification does not guarantee safety from the possibility of sin.

Third, it is not a gradual deliverance from sin. That is never God's way of victory. Sin is dealt with, settled with, done with once for all. Sin's power is broken and you yield no more.

Now having told you what it is not, let me mention three things that it is.

What it Is.

First, it is an instantaneous crisis experience. That means it has a beginning, and while you may view it as a process life-long in its result, you must also recognize its crisis nature. There must be a beginning; it must have a start. The children of Israel found the crossing of the Jordan just such an experience. It was a crisis hour in their history. In the morning they were on the wilderness side; in the evening they were on the opposite bank.

Second, it is a life of victory over sin. If it is not that, it is nothing. God has guaranteed deliverance from the power of sin. "Sin shall not have dominion over you." Apart from a life of victory over sin a profession of sanctification is a mockery.

Third, it is a life-long transformation into Christ-like-ness. "We all, with open face beholding as in a glass the glory of the Lord, are changed into the same image from glory to glory, even as by the Spirit of the Lord" (2 Cor. 3:18). More and more we partake of His image until at last when He shall appear we shall be like Him.

When Does it Take Place?

When does Sanctification take place? In God's plan at

conversion, but in man's experience, as a rule, after. I do not believe that God intends His children to wander for years in the wilderness. It is His purpose that they should yield so fully at conversion and live such a Spirit-filled life ever after that back-sliding would be unknown. Unfortunately very few do, and the result is that there must come a second great crisis when they turn from failure and disappointment in absolute surrender to live only and wholly for God.

What are the Three Steps?

There are three steps in Sanctification, and there are two parts to the experience. I am speaking now, not of the doctrinal but rather of the practical side. From a theological standpoint you may not understand it, and yet you may know it experimentally.

Now from a practical standpoint there are, as I have already stated, two sides to the experience known as Sanctification. There is first man's part and second, God's part.

A very significant statement is found in Joshua 3:5, where the command is given, "Sanctify yourselves." "But," you exclaim, "I always thought that Sanctification was a work of the Holy Spirit." Then how do you explain this very clear and definite injunction, "Sanctify yourselves"? The problem is not hard to solve. This is man's part. And before God can possibly do His part, man must do his, and sanctify himself.

I have also stated that there are three steps in Sanctification. The first two constitute man's side of the transaction, and the third, God's. These three steps, very simply worded, are: (1) Separation; (2) Dedication; (3) Filling. First "separation from," second, "dedication to," third, "filling with."

You see, it means not only a "separation from," but also a "dedication to." Separation is the negative side, dedication the positive. There are two parts to man's side of sanctification. "Sanctify yourselves." You do your part and God will do His. The third step is "filling with." But this is God's part. And the reason so many pray and plead and wait in vain for the "filling with" is simply because they have not yet taken both the steps demanded by God upon which the third depends.

Let us then first of all be sure that our separation is complete. God insists upon a clean cut separation from sin in every shape and form, from the world and all its allurements, from everything that grieves the Holy Spirit and cripples our power. Nor can we fool Him. He knows whether or not we mean what we say. Is then our separation complete? And if not let us begin at once to go all the way.

Second, we must dedicate our lives to God. Separation is incomplete unless it involves this second step. We separate from the old self life and all that is displeasing to God, only that we may be separated unto Him. Hence, dedication means the setting of one's self apart for God. We are to be holy; that is, we are separated unto God for a holy purpose. This dedication must be made actual and real in our experience.

Now, when you know positively, when you are absolutely sure that you have taken these first two steps after waiting before God long enough for the Holy Spirit to search you, then by simple faith, without any outward manifestation whatever, you can believe the Word, and rise from your knees knowing that God has done His part.

Fact, Faith, Feeling.

Now don't let Satan cheat you out of the blessing by making you wait for some supernatural manifestation or feeling. You will know the joy and comfort of the Holy Spirit as you go out believing, testifying, acting on your faith. God's order for Sanctification is the same as for Salvation. First, "fact"; second, "faith"; third, "feeling." Now Satan always reverses the Divine order, and tells you to look for feeling. But how can you feel before you believe and how can you believe until you know something to believe?

Here are some facts: "If we confess our sins, He is faithful and just to forgive us our sins, and to cleanse us from all unrighteousness" (1 John 1:9). The condition is that you confess. Have you met the condition? Then, why make God a liar? "If we walk in the light, as He is in the light, we have fellowship one with another, and the blood of Jesus Christ His Son cleanseth us from all sin" (1 John 1:7). What is the condition? "If we walk in the light." And what happens? "The blood of Jesus Christ, His Son, cleanseth us from all sin." "But," you say, "I don't feel cleansed." No, and you never will until you first of all believe God's Word and act on your faith.

So it is with Sanctification. You do your part and God will do His. You separate and dedicate and God will fill. Thus you will experience and live a Sanctified Life.

6

The Lordship of Jesus

There are many to whom Jesus Christ is Saviour but not Lord; many who have been saved by Jesus who have never recognized Him as Master. They are His children but not His disciples. A disciple is a learner, one who follows after and who recognizes another as master.

The Lord Jesus has the absolute right to lay down the terms upon which He will accept followers as His disciples. In the days of the Great War when conscription was in vogue, men were compelled to serve whether they wanted to or not, but before the days of conscription every man had the privilege of deciding for himself. Now the government had the right to lay down the terms upon which men would be enlisted as soldiers, but the man himself after reading the terms had the right to accept or reject as he saw fit. That did not mean that he was no longer a citizen of his country. It simply meant that he refused to serve.

And, so with you, my friend. You may belong to Jesus Christ and be a citizen of Heaven and still refuse to acknowledge Him as your Lord and Master and place yourself under His orders in glad obedience. You may be saved and yet not be a disciple.

God First

"He that loveth father or mother *more* than Me is not worthy of Me: and he that loveth son or daughter *more* than Me is not worthy of Me" (Matt. 10:37).

What, then, are the terms of discipleship? Let me give the answer in just two words: "GOD FIRST." And if I could, I would put them on a banner in the sight of every congregation in the world—GOD FIRST.

Now let us ask ourselves some very plain questions. Does God come first in my life or does business hold the supreme place? Is it God first or pleasure? God first or money? What about my family, my loved ones? Do they come first or does God?

Renunciation

The last condition of discipleship is found in Luke 14:33. It reads as follows: "Whosoever he be of you that forsaketh not all that he hath, he cannot be My disciple." "But," you exclaim, "that condition is almost impossible to meet. Do you mean to say that God asks His follower literally to forsake everything? If so, then I am not His disciple, for I still have a home, a wife and a small bank account. Am I to forsake these?"

In the Revised Version you will find that the word "forsake" has been translated "renounce." Now let us read it: "Whosoever he be of you that *renounceth* not all that he hath, he cannot be My disciple." It is one thing to renounce; it is another to forsake. God demands that His children renounce everything whereas He may ask them to actually forsake very few of the things they have renounced.

To renounce a thing means to relinquish all claim. Nothing that I am or own belongs to me. All is God's. He allows me the use of it as it pleases Him, but He has the first, the supreme claim. Recognizing that, I gladly place all at His disposal.

Now let me renounce all that I have. Let me lay everything on God's altar—myself, my loved ones, my talents and time, my money and my unknown future.

1. *Self.*

God does not want your money first, He wants you. He does not want your service first, He wants you. "They... first gave their own selves to the Lord" (2 Cor. 8:5).

What would a man think of a young woman who in response to his appeal, offered her lover lands and houses or anything else she owned? Would he be satisfied? Not for a moment. He is not asking for her possessions; he is asking for herself.

Nor will any substitute satisfy. And so it is with Jesus Christ. He wants us, body, soul and spirit. Hence, we must first of all lay ourselves on the altar.

> *Take myself and I will be*
> *Ever, only, all for Thee.*

2. *Loved Ones.*

Having placed myself on God's altar, I now bring my loved ones, my son or daughter, my father or mother. If the Lord wants my child for the foreign field, he may have her. If He demands that I leave father and mother, I obey. Even if He should choose to take my loved one to Himself I dare not murmur. "Thy will be done."

"Why am I not happy?" inquired a wealthy lady as she

stood in her home beside the great missionary, Dr. Jonath-
an Goforth, of China.

"Have you surrendered all?" inquired the man of God,
quietly.

"Yes, so far as I know, I have surrendered all," responded the woman.

"Are you sure," insisted Dr. Goforth, "that your all is
on the altar?"

"My all is on the altar, I believe," answered the woman
again.

"And you would be willing for God to take your little
girl here and send her to China?" asked the missionary,
placing his hand on her head.

"God take my daughter and make her a missionary in
China! I should say not. I want her here with me," exclaimed the mother.

"And yet you tell me you have surrendered all, and you
haven't even given your own child to God. How can you
expect God's peace and blessing? You stand as it were
between God and His will for your daughter, and you say
to Him, 'Thus far shalt Thou come and no farther. You can
have my home; You can have my money; You can have
me, but don't touch my daughter.' Madam, do you call
that surrender?"

3. *Talents.*

Our talents were never given to be used for ourselves.
God's gifts are to be invested for Him. What right have
we to use them selfishly? Once we catch God's vision,
never again will we use our talents along worldly lines.
You may have a talent for elocution, oratory, speaking.
The question is: How are you using it? Is it simply for

the purpose of amusing and entertaining? Or has it been invested for God? You may be gifted in writing. But what and for whom are you writing? Is it for the world, or for God? Are you writing for money or for the Kingdom? It may be you have been given the talent of making money. But remember, "It is God that giveth thee power to get wealth." Then for whom are you making money? For yourself or for God? Or your talent may be that of song. God has given you a voice. Are you using it in concerts to please your friends? Do you sing the songs of the world? Or, can Jesus Christ proclaim His message to burdened, sin sick souls, through your talent of song? Frances Ridley Havergal sang:

> *Take my voice and let me sing*
> *Always, only, for my King.*

4. *Time.*

"Redeeming the time." What a responsibility! What are we doing with our time, our spare hours? Do we invest it for God or use it for selfish pursuits that don't count? Somehow we seem to have time for everything else in the world, time to eat and time to sleep, time to shop and time to talk, time for the newspaper and time for our visitors, time for pleasure and time for work, but no time for God. Do we spend our time entertaining our friends, providing expensive dinner parties, and whiling away the hours in idle talk? Or, do we live as pilgrims and act like sojourners? Are we different from the world? Let us begin right now to practise what we sing:

> *All for Jesus! all for Jesus!*
> *All my days and all my hours.*

5. *Money.*

Not a tenth, but all. Everything we own belongs to God and we are only stewards. Then it behoves us to watch how we spend it. Does it go for luxury or for missions; for non-necessities or for the evangelization of the world? Do we spend it on ourselves to gratify our selfish desires, or is it held and used in God's work? Are we simply banking it to leave to someone who is quite able to take care of himself? Or are we investing it as God's steward in the souls of men? Not, "How much of my money will I give to God," but, "How much of God's money will I keep for myself?" Some day He will call us to account for our stewardship. Our money, then, must also be placed on God's altar.

> *Take my silver and my gold,*
> *Not a mite would I withhold.*

6. *My Unknown Future.*

All my plans and ambitions; all my dreams and aspirations—all must be laid on God's altar. He must guide, direct and control my life. His will must become my will, His programme mine. My future must be in His hands. Where He wants me to go I must go; I must have no plans of my own.

Well, now, will you lay your all on the altar? Are you ready to yield, to dedicate, to consecrate everything? Oh, that you would take this initial step! Be definite. Make a whole-hearted surrender of your life to God. Hold nothing back. Yield up your will and accept His. There can be no substitute for your act of surrender.

It is a question of signing a blank agreement. Put your

name down at the bottom and let God write in the terms and conditions of the agreement after. He will only put down one step at a time and when you take that the next will be made plain.

It means that you sail under sealed orders. Where, you do not know. When, you cannot say. Why, is not your business. How, must not concern you. It is yours to accept from Him the sealed orders containing His blueprint for your life, and to open and read them just when and just as much at a time as He wills.

It is saying an eternal "Yes" to God. An eternal "No" to self. And it must be so final that it holds good all the rest of your life. "Lord, what wilt Thou have me to do? Where wilt Thou have me to go?" He dictates and you obey. One great, final, eternal, glorious Yes, and the question is forever settled. Then just keep saying "Yes" all along the way.

Having definitely relinquished all claim, I deliberately turn my back on everything. Thus I renounce all that I am and have. It is no longer mine but God's. Henceforth He has the absolute right to do what He likes with it, and if at any time He should call upon me to literally forsake what I have renounced I must not even murmur or complain.

No sooner will I renounce all than God will test me to see if my renunciation is genuine. It was so with Abraham. He had renounced Isaac, recognizing that he belonged to God alone. Then God demanded the sacrifice on Mount Moriah and Abraham never flinched. His renunciation was thereby proven to be genuine. It will not be hard when the test comes if the renunciation has been real. But if it has only been a fake, the testing time will be terrible, and in all probability the thing that was supposed to have been renounced will be taken back. Discipleship demands renunciation.

Lord of All

Remember, Jesus must be Lord of all, or not Lord at all. No man ever works for two firms at the same time. No slave owns two masters at once. Beware lest when you give Him a secondary place as you think, you awaken some day when it is too late to discover that He is not there at all. For He must be Lord of all, or not Lord at all. "No man can serve two masters." "Suffer me first," said the young man to Jesus. Oh no, not "me first"—God First! My interests must always come second to His; never first. "Seek ye first the Kingdom of God."

Dr. Graham Scroggie, of Edinburgh, was one time speaking along this line, and at the close of the service he was approached by a young woman, a professing Christian, who had been greatly stirred.

"And why don't you yield?" inquired Dr. Scroggie.

"I am afraid I would have to do two things if I did," responded the girl.

"What are they?" questioned the minister.

"I play the piano in a concert hall, and I fear I would have to give it up," explained the inquirer. "And the other?"

"I am afraid God would send me to China as a missionary."

Dr. Scroggie was wise in his dealings with the anxious. Opening his Bible at Acts 10:14, he explained to the young woman the absurdity of Peter's answer, "Not so, Lord." A slave never dictates. And to say, "Not so," and then add the word "Lord," is impossible.

"Now," said Dr. Scroggie, "I want you to cross out the two words 'Not so' and leave the word 'Lord'; or else cross out 'Lord' and leave 'not so'."

Handing her his pencil he quietly walked away. Later he returned. Looking over her shoulder he saw a tear-stained page, but the words "Not so" were crossed out. With a glad light in her eyes she left the church and went home repeating over and over the one word, "Lord." No longer would she dictate. She was now His disciple and He her Lord and Master. Henceforth it would be, "Even so, Father," and, "Lord, what wilt Thou have me to do?"

"Lovest thou Me more than these?" And I can imagine Jesus pointing to the boats and nets, then to the other disciples, and finally to Peter's home and loved ones. "Peter, who comes first? Do I? Lovest thou Me more than these?" And that is the question He is asking still. Shall we, then, yield all, and crown Him Lord?

> *All hail the power of Jesus' Name!*
> *Let Angels prostrate fall;*
> *Bring forth the royal diadem*
> *And crown Him Lord of all.*

7

Our Most Important Work

When I was Pastor in Dale Presbyterian Church, Toronto, I had an experience that made me realize, as never before, the seriousness of my calling. It happened suddenly, and I can still remember the telephone call that aroused me from my indifference and made me hurry, to the bedside of one of my parishioners.

"Could you come to see a sick woman?"

"Is it urgent?"

"Yes, very; she may not live through the night."

"All right, I'll come at once," and I hung up the receiver.

Making my way through the city streets, I was soon at the place, and was taken immediately to the sick chamber. A woman with a sad and forlorn expression on her face looked up at me as I entered. She tried to speak, but her voice was so weak and broken that I had to bend low to catch the words she uttered. And I felt that I was already standing in the presence of the Angel of Death, for it was plain to see that her life was fast ebbing away.

Hopelessness was depicted on her countenance while she waited for me to speak; and the darkness seemed to deepen as I watched the pale, drawn face, enshrouded in the gloom of almost hopeless despair. There was no time to lose—no time to talk of the things of this world: her eternal destiny was at stake.

"Mrs. Cook, are you ready to go; have you any hope?" I enquired, as I bent over her.

"No, none," she murmured, shaking her head, while a deep drawn sigh escaped her lips.

I stated as plainly as I could the wonderful plan of salvation, and, kneeling down, prayed with her, and then sang in tones subdued and low:

> *Just as I am—without one plea,*
> *But that Thy blood was shed for me,*
> *And that Thou bidd'st me come to Thee,*
> *O Lamb of God, I come!*
>
> *Just as I am—and waiting not*
> *To rid my soul of one dark blot,*
> *To Thee, whose blood can cleanse each spot,*
> *O Lamb of God, I come!*

As I sang the second verse, I heard her feeble voice broken, weak and wavering trying to sing with me. Sometimes I could distinguish the words, but more often they were unintelligible, until I came to the last line, and then she sang with heart and voice: *"O Lamb of God, I come!"* And she did come—came in full assurance of faith; and I left her, knowing that all was well, and that she was going home to God.

And yet she was a member of the church, a member but unconverted. Conversion was her one great need, for the Word of God plainly and emphatically states that, "Except ye be converted, ye shall not enter into the kingdom of heaven" (Matt. 18:3). And as I went home, my heart was sad within me, and I groaned aloud as I thought of the awful responsibility resting upon ministers who allow people to become members of churches without being "born again."

I never saw Mrs. Cook again until I stood by her casket and looked down upon her face, cold in death. And as I preached her funeral sermon, I determined more than ever to lay aside everything else and give myself unreservedly to the one great work of getting people ready for Heaven.

Soul-winning

The more I study God's Word the more I am convinced that our most important work is the winning of lost men and women to Jesus Christ. Among many others there are four outstanding passages that clearly set forth this great fact.

First, looking at it from God's side, we find that "Christ Jesus came into the world to save sinners" (1 Tim. 1:15), that "the Son of Man is come to seek and to save that which is lost" (Luke 19:10). Hence the supreme purpose of Christ's coming to this world was to seek and to save the lost. Not a mission of Social Service and Reformation, but of Salvation and Regeneration.

Then from man's side it is, "to open their eyes, and to turn them from darkness to light, and from the power of Satan unto God" (Acts 26:18). Men are in darkness; they must have their eyes opened and be led into the light. They are under the power of Satan; and hence, they must be delivered and brought to God.

Then the whole purpose is summed up plainly and unmistakably in Acts 15:14, where it is stated that God visited the Gentiles "to take out of them a people for His name." That is what God has been doing for the past 1900 years. This is the work of the Holy Spirit today. He is gathering out the Body of Christ, His Church. From every race and tongue the world over He is calling out this great company.

Now, if such is God's purpose in visiting the Gentiles, and He declares that it is: and if this is the mission of the Holy Spirit in the world, then it is God's will that we should co-operate with Him—for He works through human instruments   and seek to do our part in gathering out His Church.

There are some people who shift the responsibility of soul winning by saying that "one sows and another reaps." Well, suppose you sow a beautiful garden and in the fall of the year someone comes around and sees it. "Now, my friend," he says, "you have done your part, you faithfully did the sowing; and now the time has come for the reaping. I will begin to reap, to gather all these vegetables and this fruit that you have sowed. One sows, you know, and another reaps."

"Oh, no," you exclaim, "I should say not! I sowed this garden for myself. Do you mean to say that I am going to let you have all the fruit of my labour? I will reap it myself." And so you do; for the explanation that "one sows and another reaps" holds good—according to this argument in the spiritual realm only.

But God clearly and emphatically states that it is His will that every servant of His should bear fruit. "I have chosen you and ordained you," He affirms, "that ye should go and bring forth fruit" (John 15:16). Sometimes I am the one who sows, but at other times I am the one who reaps as well.

Side-tracked by Satan

If soul winning is the most important work of the church, it naturally follows that Satan will do all he can to get us side tracked or satisfied with something else. Thousands therefore are giving themselves to Social Service, including education, philanthropy and reform work, etc. But Social Service is not Salvation; and Reformation is not Regeneration. One has to do with this life, the other with Eternity.

If we would gauge the spiritual life of a church we must do it by ascertaining its attitude toward the perishing. The Annual Report may tell of a great work done and a large amount of money raised for benevolent purposes, but if it has no record to give of souls won, its spiritual life is low indeed. Real spirituality always results in soul winning.

This, then, is our most important work. And what a glorious occupation! How wonderful to be linked up with God in the greatest of all undertakings! Oh, my brethren, let us get back, back to our old-time love for the lost! Where, oh where, is the burden of bygone years? How earnestly we once prayed for perishing souls! How eagerly we watched for results! Have we lost all feeling? Does the awful doom of the unconverted no longer move us? Has Satan so far side tracked us that we have forgotten our most important work?

Oh, then, if that be so, may God in His great mercy open our eyes, and get us off the side-tracks so cunningly laid by Satan, back to our most important work, the winning of souls to Jesus Christ.

8

The Investment of Life

God has a plan for every life. He had a plan for Jeremiah's life even before he saw the light of day (Jer. 1:5). He has a plan for your life; He has one for mine. And because of this fact no one can be supremely happy until he has found God's plan for his life. Are you ever discontented, despondent, or miserable? It may be that you have refused to accept His plan and have persisted in following one of your own. But you ask: "How am I to know God's plan?" That I cannot answer. You must decide it for yourself. I may, however, by God's help, be able to make it easier for you to reach a decision.

As a follower of the Lord Jesus Christ you have but one great aim, i.e., the advancement of God's kingdom. As a Christian, I say, the interests of the kingdom of God become your main object in life. God's work is of paramount importance. Everything else must take a secondary place. Jesus Christ never entrusted this work to the ministers alone; He has laid it upon every Christian man, upon every Christian woman. Each individual believer has his own particular part. God is depending upon you; He is depending upon me. He trusts us. If, then, our aim is to serve the kingdom of God it necessarily follows that:

Service is the Highest Motive

Not dollars and cents, but service. The man who measures success in life by the standpoint of money has not caught the true meaning of success. There is another standard, vastly higher. Oh, that we might catch the vision of that standard!

Let us listen to the warning voice of the Master Himself as He exclaims, "Take heed, and beware of covetousness, for a man's life consisteth not in the abundance of the things which he possesseth" (Luke 12:15).

The majority of you who read this message are intending to spend your lives in the business world. You believe that in this way you can best serve the interests of the kingdom. Probably you are right. It is not for me to act as judge. All that I ask is that you invest your life in terms of service. In other words, if you can best serve God's kingdom as a merchant, then be a merchant; as a lawyer, be a lawyer; as a stenographer, be a stenographer; as a doctor, then by all means be a doctor. God has so ordained it that money is necessary to carry on His work. It may be that He would have you assist in this capacity. But woe unto the man, and woe unto the woman who makes money the aim rather than the means, and piles it up for selfish purposes rather than using it for the glory of God! Beware lest you offer Him money when He is asking for life!

But possibly you are still young. Then to you I would speak especially, for there lies before you a great field of opportunity and responsibility, and you are just on the eve of choosing your life's work. Oh, that I might guide you in your choice! So much depends upon your view of a successful career. You have a life to invest. You desire to invest it as God has planned you should. But the way seems dark. There are so many things that you might do that it seems extremely difficult to decide. Is there no help in such a crisis, no guiding star? I think there is. It seems to me that in the investment of life the place of greatest need has first claim.

Do we need more business men today, or do we need more ministers, more lawyers or more foreign missionaries; more doctors in this country or more in Africa and India? Do we need more lady stenographers here, or more workers in the Far East? We are surely all agreed that the business world is not suffering as these other places are. I would turn your eyes to the fields that are pleading for workers because the need is greater there than anywhere else.

The Ministry

Take, for instance, the Ministry. How great is the need here! Oh, young men, do you want a field of real service, a service that will yield a rich reward? Then turn to the Ministry. It needs you, and it may be that you need it. I know of no calling that gives quite as much joy. Nor have I ever been sorry that I chose the Ministry as my life's work.

Why do you not become a minister of the Gospel? Is it because it has never occurred to you that you might? Do you look upon the Ministry as too high and sacred for you? Then remember that it is made up of ordinary men just like yourself, who have responded to the Call of God. Or is it because you have been in the habit of measuring success by the standard of dollars and cents? I grant you that a minister may never become rich as a minister. But do you mean to tell me that D. L. Moody was not a success simply because he never became wealthy; that Charles H. Spurgeon's life was a failure because he died a poor man? God help us to get rid of such a standard! Success can never be measured in dollars and cents; it can only be judged in terms of service.

The Mission Field

And now what of the Foreign Field? I almost hesitate to speak of it; but I must say a few words. And may God help me to say something that will reach every heart!

I take up a book descriptive of the conditions existing in the non-Christian world, and my heart burns within me as I read of the terrible darkness. Two-thirds of the world still without Christ! Thousands dying every day who have never heard the name of Jesus. Africa, "the open sore of the world," with her two hundred millions calling for labourers! India, the land of little widows and child-wives, with her four hundred and fifty million, stretching out weary hands for the Light until she has grown so tired that she doesn't care!

And yet the Saviour's last command was, "Go ye into all the world and preach the Gospel to every creature." Nineteen hundred years have rolled away, and we have not obeyed it yet. O young men, yes, and young women, too, for I speak to you as well, if you want a life of service and sacrifice, but also of untold joy, then I call upon you to respond to the cry that comes from over the seas. You haven't a single talent that God cannot use out there.

If there is one excuse that is given more than another on the part of young women, it is this: "I am needed at home." Or very frequently her mother will say: "Oh, we couldn't possibly get along without her; we need her at home." Listen! There comes a time when her hand is sought in marriage. You give her up. Somehow she is not needed at home any more; at least she can be spared and she goes away. What have you done? You have given her to an earthly bridegroom, and refused the Heavenly Bridegroom. Jesus, your Saviour—her Saviour—wooed and won her first. Then He tenderly asked her to follow Him. You answered: "No, Lord, I cannot spare her." Later came the earthly bridegroom, and—well, you know the rest. I wonder what you will say when you meet Him! Do you remember that He said: "He that loveth father or mother more than Me is not worthy of Me, and he that loveth son or daughter more than Me is not worthy of Me"? (Matt. 10:37).

God's Call

Young men and women, I call you this day to Christian service. I have only pointed out two great and needy fields; there are scores of others. The question resolves itself into this: Are you willing to accept God's plan for your life? If so, you will invest your life in terms of service, and you will endeavour to find the place of greatest need. Jesus gave up all for us. Is there nothing we can give to Him? God had only one Son, and He made Him a missionary. Is there nothing we can do in return?

He Himself has taught us what it means to be a true disciple when He says: "If any man will come after Me, let him deny himself, and take up his cross and follow Me.

For whosoever will save his life shall lose it; and whosoever will lose his life for My sake shall find it. For what is a man profited if he shall gain the whole world, and lose his own soul?" (Matt. 16:24-26).

9

Go and Tell Others

It is eventide. The last lingering ray of the setting sun has sunk below the horizon. The suffocating heat of the day has been replaced by the cooler air of the approaching night. The long, dark shadows cast by the city walls have disappeared. Twilight covers all.

Ever and anon from somewhere within the walls comes a faint plaintive cry. It is probably the cry of a child, caused by the pangs of hunger, for Samaria is undergoing a siege. The Syrians have laid waste the country, and surrounded the city. Days have passed, food has grown scarce, and relief seems farther off than at the beginning.

Upon this particular evening four lepers might have been seen seated on the ground just outside the wall. So weak are they that they can scarcely move. The last scrap of food has been eaten. They have reached their extremity, for when the morrow dawns, it will mean certain death. What are they to do? If they enter the city it will avail them nothing, for food can no longer be had. To remain where they are will mean starvation. Death if they go! Death if they stay! What is to be done? Is there no alternative? Ah, yes! they can give themselves up to the Syrians. True, they may be killed. But then again they may not. It is only a chance in a hundred, but life is dear even to lepers, and they decide to take the chance. Dragging themselves wearily across the open space as the twilight deepens, they finally reach the outskirts of the camp. All is still and quiet. Not a footstep is heard. What can it mean? Cautiously they make their way from tent to tent. Not a human soul. The Syrians have fled. Yes, fled, and left everything behind them. Food is found in abundance and they are saved.

Like hungry wolves they fall upon the stores, and fairly gorge themselves ere they give any thought to other things. Finally, when they have feasted as only the hungry can, they are suddenly conscience stricken by the thought of the thousands within the city walls who are dying of starvation while food is within their grasp.

"Then they said to one another, we do not well; this day is a day of good tidings, and we hold our peace; if we tarry till the morning light, punishment will overtake us; now, therefore, come, let us go and tell the King's household" (2 Kings 7:9). And with hearts grateful for the good things that had come to them, they decided to let the others know. This they did and the city was saved. Hence, our theme, "Go and tell others."

Go and tell others! It is the message that Christ Himself gave to His Church when He said, "Go into all the world and preach the Gospel." It is His will for every Christian. And I believe were He here today, in the face of the millions who have never heard His name, His most urgent plea to you and me would be this: "Go and tell others."

First, because of what we have

These four lepers had about all they wanted for the present. They had been starving and had been given food. They had been hopeless and had been filled with new aspirations. They had been sad and discouraged; they were now glad and happy. Was it any wonder that they exclaimed, "We do not well; this day is a day of good tidings, and we hold our peace"?

But, brethren, what had they in comparison to what you and I have in Jesus Christ? Their salvation was physical and temporal. Ours is spiritual and eternal. They had been freed from the pangs of hunger. We have been freed from the power of sin. Think of it!—forgiven, our hearts cleansed by the blood of Jesus Christ, the presence of God ever with us, joy, peace, comfort, the hope of life beyond the grave, re-union with those we loved and lost awhile, Heaven with all its glories, and best of all Jesus Christ Himself, our Comforter in sorrow, our Guide in the darkness, and our Strength and Hope in death. Surely, surely we have something worth giving to others! Are we going to be selfish? Would we keep it all for ourselves? Or will we do as these poor lepers did for a starving city? Will we go and tell others?

Second, because of what they need

Within the walls of Samaria were literally thousands of men and women dying of hunger. So dire was the situation, so pressing the need, that mothers were cooking their own sons that they might live a little longer. Could we imagine a greater need? Food was worth its weight in gold, and it was food they needed. And the lepers, knowing it, decided to go and tell them.

My friends, there are men and women on every side who are perishing for the Bread of Life, and we are able to supply their need. It may be that the man who works by

our side day after day does not know Jesus Christ, and we
have never told him. Take, for instance, the friends with
whom we associate. We, ourselves, have heard the "Glad
Tidings" and Jesus has become our Saviour. But what of
them? Have we ever told them what Jesus means to us?
Have we ever tried to supply their need?

Far away across the sea, there are millions of precious
souls for whom He died. And yet they have never heard
His name. Shall we not go and tell them? The last great
command of the One whom we love and serve was "Go."
And yet nineteen centuries have rolled away, and still the
world is unevangelized.

Third, because there is danger if we fail

I mean danger to ourselves. Hear the warning as we turn
to our text: "If we tarry till the morning light, punishment
will overtake us." Ah, yes! They dare not tarry. They dare
not withhold the "Glad Tidings." Some kind of punishment would surely overtake them if they did. And so without any more hesitation they went at once to tell others.

The Gospel has come to us, and through the atoning
blood of Jesus Christ we are saved. But listen, we keep it
at our peril. We must either go backward or forward. We
cannot stand still. The secret of growth in the Christian
life is activity. If we lie down and do nothing for Christ
we will grow weaker and weaker, until at last our interest will be gone. One of the greatest prerequisites of the
Christian life is service. We must go to work for Christ.
We were not saved merely that we might escape Hell and
get to Heaven. That is pure selfishness. No! No! We were
saved to serve.

There are thousands of Christians, I am sorry to say, who never speak a word for their Master. In the testimony meeting they are silent, though their tongues fly fast enough at home. They can talk to their fellow men, but somehow when it comes to speaking for God they are utterly and hopelessly dumb. They have loved ones in their own homes who do not know Christ, and yet they are afraid to say a word to them.

Unless we go and tell others we ourselves will grow cold and indifferent. Our reward will go to another, and we will suffer unutterable loss. "When I say unto the wicked, thou shalt surely die; and thou givest him not a warning, nor speakest to warn the wicked from his wicked way, to save his life; the same wicked man shall die in his iniquity; but his blood will I require at thine hand" (Ezek. 3:18). Oh, how solemn the warning, "his blood will I require at thine hand"!

"We do not well," exclaimed the lepers, "let us go and tell." Oh, my brethren, let us also go and tell. The world is dying for our message. Souls are perishing without Christ. It is for each one of us to go and tell others.

10

Seven Questions of Vital Importance

There are seven questions that every Christian should face, questions of such vital importance that to ignore them is to imperil one's spiritual life. Let us consider them, then, one by one, and may God help us to answer them honestly and sincerely.

1. *Am I Committing any known Sin?*

"If I regard iniquity in my heart the Lord will not hear me" (Ps. 66:18). He will not even listen to what I say. Hence, my prayers will not be answered while I am harbouring sin.

Note, if you will, that I have said "known" sin, for it may be that you have to face what the Bible terms "the sin that doth so easily beset us," some one sin to which, from time to time, you yield. It may be but a weight, an idol, and yet it is sin, and God says you must give it up.

"Your iniquities have separated between you and your God, and your sins have hid His face from you, so that He will not hear" (Isa. 59:2). Sin separates. Sin hides God's face. There can be no communion, no fellowship where there is sin.

"Let every one that nameth the name of Christ depart from iniquity" (2 Tim. 2:19).

That is God's command. We must forsake all known sin if we are to be approved of Him. Oh, then, let us turn from everything we know to be wrong, everything that grieves the Holy Spirit. Let us put it out of our lives, for we will never make any progress in the Christian life until we break with sin.

Sin is like a millstone; it will always hold us down. And if we yield to it, we will crave it again. To feed desire is to fan it into a flame that can never be quenched. The only real sorrow that can ever come into the life of a Christian is the torture and anguish of the heart that harbours sin.

Therefore let us break with it, break with it at all costs, or we will never know "the peace of God that passeth all understanding." Sin will ruin us unless we give it up. "The way of transgressors is hard."

"Remember Jesus Christ." He can break every fetter and snap every chain. He can set the prisoner free. And He can set you free, yes, even from your besetting sin. Not only is He mighty to save; He is also able to keep. You can be victorious over every known sin by the power of His indwelling Spirit. It pays to be an "Overcomer."

2. Am I Living in Obedience to God's Will?

"Yield yourselves unto God" (Rom. 6:13). Have I surrendered all? I sing it, I know. Again and again I exclaim, "Have Thine own way, Lord," but do I really mean it? Will I go where He wants me to go? Or do I still want my own way? And do I put self first instead of Christ? Is He the Lord and Master of my life?

God must have obedient children. If we are self-willed He cannot use us. "To obey is better than sacrifice." Rebellion in the camp is fatal to the cause. Loyalty He must have. Blunders are permissible; mistakes will be over-looked, but disloyalty—never!

If we are to be used of God we must be obedient. We must be prepared to go where God wants us to go. It must be His way instead of our own, His choice rather than ours. And, blessed be God, when we really yield to Him, His plan becomes ours, and we delight to do His will.

Let us not think of Him as a hard task-master; One who insists on us doing things we don't want to do. Not at all. He is our Father. He loves to lead us to the still waters. Within our hearts He puts the very desires that are pleasing to Him. All He asks is that we yield, for we are His, body, soul and spirit. Hence, there can be no fellowship apart from obedience.

3. *Am I Spending Time each Day in Prayer?*

No one can be victorious apart from prayer. No one can make a success of the Christian life unless he prays. If you have neglected prayer you are weak. It is those who wait upon the Lord who renew their strength. Unless you have been living, therefore, in an atmosphere of prayer you are open to the attacks of the enemy. Jesus prayed. He spent whole nights in prayer. Paul prayed. The Early Church prayed. All those who have been used of God have been men and women of prayer.

So, let me ask myself the question, do I pray? Do I keep tryst with God? Have I an appointment with Him day by day and am I careful to keep it? Does God know me as a man of prayer? Or have I failed Him? If so, may He enable me to renew my covenant and begin again to meet Him morning by morning, lest He come and find me sleeping.

4. *Am I a Diligent Student of God's Word?*

To neglect the Word of God is to cut myself off from hearing His voice, for God speaks through His Word. Hence, if I am not giving time to Bible Study I am without guidance. Many a man has gone astray simply because he has ignored the Word of God. Nothing can take its place. It is God's Word to man, and if I really know Him I will want to study it. And the more I read it the more interesting it will become. I will find that I cannot do without it. It will be my meat and my drink for the day's work.

Again and again I turned to it in the early days of my Christian life. When I was first converted I read it daily. But—am I still poring over its pages? Is it just as new to me now as it was the first time I read it? Do I revel in the experiences of the apostles and prophets? Am I still finding comfort from the Psalms of David? Is the Word of God a living Book to me, and am I feeding on it daily?

Perhaps I am weak. God compares His Word to milk and meat. Hence, if I am to be strong I must turn to it constantly.

May He enable me, therefore, to become a diligent student of His Word.

5. *Am I Confessing Christ Publicly?*

During the early years of my Christian experience I was on fire for souls. I enjoyed getting out on the street corner with a company of God's people and giving my testimony. I revelled in the opportunity of working in rescue missions and pointing souls to Christ. I was burdened about the condition of the unsaved. In the glow of my first love for Christ I eagerly sought to tell others what He had done for me. I went home to my friends even as the demoniac of old.

But what about today? Have I lost my first love? Have I become cold and indifferent? Does the fire of God no longer burn in my heart? Can I attend church and go through religious performances without any burden concerning the lost? If so, why? What has happened? I sing, "Rescue the perishing," but do I do anything to rescue them? I sing, "Care for the dying," but do I care for them? And when I join in the words, "Weep o'er the erring one," are my eyes dry or do I actually weep over the perishing? Have I any heart interest in the salvation of lost men and women? If not, there is something seriously the matter, and I should start at once to discover the cause and remedy it. I must confess Christ publicly. I must make Him known. He has commanded me to bear witness. Let me again, therefore, testify. Surely, I can distribute gospel tracts. Surely, I can write soul-winning letters to my friends. At least I can speak to those with whom I work. If I am God's representative, I must be true.

6. *Am I Giving Liberally as God Prospers Me?*

"Give, and it shall be given unto you" (Luke 6:38).

As we give God gives, for He will be no man's debtor. You cannot beat God giving. One tenth at least should be set aside for God's work, and then as much more as He asks. For if you are faithful with Him He will be faithful to you. The reason so many are destitute today is because they did not play square with God when they had plenty. Seldom will you find one who has faithfully given to God's work in a systematic way through the years of prosperity who is in want. "The liberal soul shall be made fat, and he that watereth shall be watered also himself" (Prov. 11:25).

But when you do give, be sure you are giving to a definite, soul-winning work, and not to Social Service or Modernism. For God will hold you responsible to find out how your gifts are being used.

And give cheerfully, for "the Lord loveth a cheerful giver." Give systematically, month by month, or week by week. Keep books with God. But however you give, give, for "how shall they hear except they be sent?" If the Gospel is to be given to the world someone must pay the bill. It is like water. The water is free, but you have to pay for the piping. And so with salvation. It costs to send it on its way, and we must speed it to the uttermost part of the earth. Hence, in the language of the apostle Paul, giving becomes a Christian grace, and if we are New Testament Christians, we will give and give liberally.

7. *Am I Doing Something Definite for the Lord Jesus Christ?*

If I am to be used of God I must find a place and a people where I can give my testimony and not feel that I am condemned by those around me. A soul winning church must become my home. I am saved to serve, and unless I am doing something for the Lord Jesus I am not true to the vision He has given me. I may not have many talents, but I can do something. I can visit the sick, I can distribute gospel tracts, I can testify, I can do personal work. I can do something.

There are those who wait to be asked. They attend the church, enjoy the services, but never think of taking part themselves. They have an idea that the pastor will seek them out if he needs them and tell them what to do. It seems to me, however, that if they are really saved they will find something themselves. Paul's first cry was, "Lord, what wilt Thou have me to do?" And that ought to be the cry of every new-born soul. Love is service, and those who really love the Lord Jesus will want to serve Him. They will never be satisfied to be drones.

Instead of waiting for their pastor or someone to tell them what to do, they will go direct to God and get their instructions from Him. It may be He will want them to teach a Sunday School class. If so, they will approach the superintendent and offer their services. If they have a voice they will be eager to sing in the choir, or if there is an orchestra and they can play an instrument, they will play.

Some may be called to usher, others to serve in the Young People's organizations, or as intercessors. It may be that the foreign field is calling, and that there is an urge to train and prepare for whole-time service. One thing is certain: they will never be at rest if they have been truly born again until they are doing something for the Lord Jesus Christ.

These, then, are the questions that must be faced if we are to receive His approbation. "Study to show thyself approved unto God," is His Word, "a workman that needeth not to be ashamed." For if we would receive a full reward; if we would hear Him say, "Well done, good and faithful servant," we must examine ourselves and see to it that we measure up to His requirements.

11

The Fourfold Need of the New Life

A little baby has been born. A new life has come. You care for it. You wash it and dress it. You feed it and warm it. Day after day you attend to its needs. You know that it cannot take care of itself.

You have been born into the Kingdom of God. You opened your heart to Jesus Christ and invited Him in. You received Him as your Saviour, and now you are His. And when He came He gave you eternal life. You now have a life that you never had before, viz., *God*-life, *divine*-life. "I give unto them *eternal* life."

Well now, how are you going to take care of that new life? You are a babe in Christ. What then are the needs of the new life? Much the same as the needs of a baby.

1. *Food.*

A baby must be fed, and fed daily. So must you. That new life that God has given you requires food. The food for a baby is milk. The food of a spiritual babe is the milk of the Word. "As newborn babes, desire the sincere milk of the Word, that ye may grow thereby."

I was converted in 1906. From that day to this I have read God's Word every day of my life, three hundred and sixty-five days of the year. I cannot remember a single day when I have neglected the Book of books. The Bible has been my meat and my drink all down the years, and the more I study it the more precious it becomes. There is no book like it. When Satan's attacks have been unusually severe, God's Word has been my comfort and my stay. Time after time it has been in very deed His Word to me. Trials that might have terminated my ministry have been frustrated by the promises of God's Word.

When sorrow has overwhelmed my soul and tragedy engulfed me, God has spoken to me from the Scriptures. In the midst of my bitterest disappointment, I have heard His voice: "Weeping may endure for a night, but joy cometh in the morning." And when my heart was filled with fear, I heard Him say, "Why art thou cast down, O my soul? and why art thou disquieted in me? Hope thou in God: for I shall yet praise Him." And I found Him true.

2. *Fellowship.*

The baby needs fellowship. It must be able to express itself and make known its needs. When it is hungry or in pain, it cries. And the mother immediately answers.

You, too, need fellowship. And if you are rightly born there will be a cry in your heart. We call that cry prayer. And I would urge you to get alone with God every day of your life and pray. Tell Him all. Hide nothing. Talk to Him as you would talk to a friend.

When you read the Bible God talks to you, when you pray you talk to Him, and thus you have fellowship. You become acquainted with God exactly as you become acquainted with a friend. You speak and He speaks. And as you talk you get to know each other. Oh then, talk much to God. Pray.

3. *Exercise.*

That little baby needs exercise. It shoves out its little legs and arms in order to exercise them.

You, too, need exercise if you are to grow strong. And so you must bear witness to Christ, for that is the way you exercise. Tell others. Do personal work. Confess Christ publicly. Witness. If you don't, you will backslide. If you do, you will become strong. Get busy and do something for Christ. You will if you truly love Him. "Let the redeemed of the Lord say so." Refuse to be silent. If you appreciate what He has done for you, you will not hesitate to say so.

You should at least be as proud of your Lord and Saviour as you are of your king and country. You would not be ashamed to show your colours on the battlefield. As a matter of fact, you would be eager to unfurl your country's flag and march under it. Then why should you hesitate to lift up the banner of King Jesus? For thus you can let the world know which side you are on. Do you want Him to be ashamed of you in that Great Day, ashamed before His Father and the angels? Then you must not be ashamed of Him now. God says, "With the mouth confession is made unto salvation" (Rom. 10:10).

Nothing can strengthen the believer like open confession. If you want to grow spiritually confess Christ publicly. Satan doesn't mind silent Christians, but he objects most strenuously to those who openly declare their allegiance to Christ. Yet the very act of confession renders powerless his attacks.

You can talk about the one you love. At least, most people can. And if you really and truly love the Lord Jesus

Christ you will want to talk about Him.

And testimony, my friend, is the best antidote there is to worldly companionship. You will never have to give them up, those worldly friends of yours, never. Just tell them about Jesus. Ask them to kneel down while you pray with them. Hand them a gospel tract, and invite them to an evangelistic service. Try it. Do you know what will happen? They will drop you like a hot coal. You will no longer be wanted. And then you will find new friends and associates, Christians, who will love what you love, and want what you want. And their friendship will be yours through all Eternity. Even death cannot sever such a relationship.

Oh, then, let us be true to God. Let us testify of Christ. Let us confess Him publicly before men, and the joy and approbation of the Lord will be our reward.

4. *Atmosphere*.

No mother would put her new-born babe in a refrigerator. She sees that the room is neither too cold nor too hot. The atmosphere must be exactly what it needs.

If you go to a dead, cold, formal church, you will freeze.

If you go to a modernistic church, you will starve. But if you go to a church where the invitation is given and souls are saved, if you attend evangelistic meetings where they sing gospel hymns, if you go where they pray and testify, you will find yourself in an atmosphere exactly suited to your needs. It is up to you to find a group of God's people on fire for souls.

Hence, my exhortation is not, join the church, but, link up with a soul-saving, missionary centre. Work only with a company of people that love the Lord, a people who will welcome your testimony for Christ, and where your voice can be raised in prayer and supplication. Don't compromise. If you do it will be at the peril of your spiritual life.

And be sure that the man who occupies the pulpit believes in the fundamentals of the Faith. Make certain that he preaches the blood, that he recognizes that men are lost and need to be saved, and that he insists on the new birth.

Avoid worldly churches. God wants a separated people. "Be not unequally yoked," He says, "with unbelievers."

These, then, are the needs of the new life, and the responsibility rests on you. Therefore, take care of it. Feed it. Give it fellowship. Exercise it. And provide the atmosphere it requires. Then you will go on with God and the Christian life will be all that was promised.

12

The Morning Watch

In the very early years of my Christian life I commenced observing what I have called the "Morning Watch." Every morning, day in and day out, I get alone with God. I would not dream of going to my office before first of all spending time alone with Him. Nor would I attempt to carry on my church work without first meeting God, morning by morning. Directly after breakfast I retire to my study, close the door, and there spend the first hour alone with God. For over 70 years now I have observed the Morning Watch. If God has used me in any way down through the years it is because I have met Him morning by morning. I solve my problems before I come to them. Without the Morning Watch my work would be ineffective. I would be weak and helpless. It is only when I wait upon Him that I become strong spiritually.

You Must Make Time.

You tell me that you do not have time; you are so busy in the work of the Lord that you cannot spare an hour to wait upon Him. Well, Susanna Wesley was busy. She had nineteen children, you remember. And in those days they did not have schools. She had to teach them herself. She could not go to the stores to buy clothes for them. She had to make them. Moreover, she had to provide their daily food. Yet Susanna Wesley every day from one o'clock until two went into her bedroom, closed the door, and there on her knees spent the time alone with God. No child dare interrupt her during that hour. They all knew what she was doing. No wonder Susanna Wesley gave the world John Wesley and Charles Wesley. She knew what is was to get alone with God.

My friend, if Susanna Wesley, busy as she was, mother of nineteen children, could make time to wait upon God, surely you and I, in this day of gadgets, can do the same. We will never get time; we will have to make time. And unless we make time we will not accomplish very much for God.

That is the way we become acquainted with our friends; we take time to meet them, and thus we get to know them. When a young man wants to get married he makes a date, I suppose, with the young woman of his choice. It is hard, of course, for him to spare the time. He realizes that it will mean sacrifices on his part. But, nevertheless, he makes up his mind that it must be done. Somehow or other he must spend an hour or two in her company if he is going to become acquainted with her. He sets aside a certain evening and arranges to call on her. Everything else has to be laid aside, and in spite of the tremendous sacrifice he is making he bravely prepares for the interview. She ushers him into her living room and he sits on one side and she sits on the other side. They never say a word. They just sit there and look at each other. After an hour and a half has passed he says to her, "Well, I guess it's time for me to go now. It's getting late it's almost ten o'clock." She gives him his hat and his coat and he takes his departure.

Is that the way it is? Not when I was young. She says something to him. He says something to her. They talk to one another. They enjoy each other's company. They look forward with great eagerness to the next meeting, and thus they become acquainted.

So it is with the Lord Jesus Christ. It is so important that you must make time if you are going to become acquainted with Him. Thousands there are who have met the Lord Jesus Christ who do not know Him. You have to live with people in order to know them. I met Haile Selassie, the Emperor of Ethiopia. I shook hands with him and photographed him when I was in Africa. I met the Crown Prince, and also the little prince. He came running toward me, begging me to take his picture, as I had taken the picture of his royal father. But I do not know Haile Selassie. I have never lived with him. I have only met him. You met the Lord Jesus Christ when you were converted, but unless you have taken time to become acquainted with Him you do not know Him.

Sometimes you wonder why you cannot rush into God's presence in an hour of need and get His ear. You would never dream of going to a stranger in time of trouble. If you do not know God, and He seems afar off, how can you turn to Him? You have never become acquainted with Him. However, if you have learned to know Him, if you are intimate with Him, then, in your hour of tragedy, you can turn to Him at a moment's notice and He will answer. It will be the most natural thing in the world for you to confide in Him, but you must first know Him. And to know Him takes time. You will have to make time if you are going to become acquainted with Him.

Now how do I observe the Morning Watch? Well, first of all I study the Word, and then I pray.

The Word of God.

First, then, I turn to the Word of God. Do you do that? Has there ever been a day in your life since you were converted when you have neglected the Book of books? Have you opened it every day of your life and pored over its sacred pages? Or have there been days when you have failed to read it? I would never dream of going through a day without seeking guidance from God's Word. It is my meat and my drink. Here is my authority: "As new-born babes, desire the sincere milk of the word, that ye may grow thereby" (1 Pct. 2:2).

One day, just after I had accepted Christ as my Saviour, I was standing at the back of Cooke's Presbyterian Church, Toronto. A personal worker stepped up to me and asked me to loan him my Bible. I did so. He turned to the fly-leaf and he wrote these words: "This Book will keep you from sin, or sin will keep you from this Book." Then he handed it back to me. I think I have written that statement in every Bible I have owned from that day to this, for I found it to be true. Later, I discovered that the one who had originally penned it was the immortal John Bunyan, and after that I signed his name to the statement. The fact of the matter is, sin and the Book cannot co-exist. You will either give up one or the other. If you read the Word of God, you will turn away from sin. If you indulge in sin, you will have no appetite for the Book. "This Book will keep you from sin, or sin will keep you from this Book."

My Bible.

May I suggest that you get a Bible with large type, because the day will come when your eyes will grow dim, and then, if you have carefully marked your Bible, you will be glad that the print is large enough for you to still read it. You will not want to cast it aside. Of course, you should always read with a pencil in hand. My Bibles have been marked from Genesis to Revelation. I mark every verse that speaks to my heart. You, too, should mark your Bible.

All down the years of my ministry I have used a Scofield Reference Bible. I have found it more valuable by far than any other. I do not agree with all the notes, but I do agree with most of them, and they have been a wonderful help to me in my Bible study. If I had no other books, I could take a Scofield Reference Bible and travel the world over, and I would have all the sermons I could possibly preach. The Scofield Reference Bible is the King James Version. That version has never been displaced by another, and I doubt very much if it ever will be. It speaks to the heart. Other versions are good to use as references, but if I were you I would stick to the King James Version for my own devotional reading.

You Find it Dry.

You tell me that the Bible is dry and uninteresting, and that that is why you don't read it. May I say that the reason you find it dry and uninteresting is because you do not know the Author. As I have already stated, you have met the Author, but you have not become acquainted with Him. Once you really know Him you will enjoy everything that has come from Him.

There was one time a young woman who tried to read a book of poems. She found them so dry and uninteresting, however, that she threw them aside. Later on she met the young man who had written them and fell in love with him. Then once again she picked up the book of poems, and this time, to her utter amazement and astonishment, she found them the most interesting poems she had ever read in her life. What made the difference? They were still the same dry poems they had been before. The difference was in her, not in the poems. She had now met the author, and as she read them she thought of him.

So will it be with you. If you know the Author, the Lord Jesus Christ, you will revel in His Word. It will mean more to you than any other book. The more you read it, the more you will want to read it. There are very few books that I can read more than once. There are a few that I have read twice. There are one or two that I have read three times. Worldly books lose their interest simply because they are written by human beings and are easily understood.

The Word of God is entirely different. It is supernatural. It has come from God. I can never sound its depths. There is always something new in it, something I have not seen before. The more I read it, the more I enjoy it. When I read the Old Testament I read about men whom I am going to see one of these days, and so I want to learn all I can about them. Therefore I find the Old Testament fascinating as well as the New.

How Should You Read it?

Moreover, I read it daily, just as the children of Israel gathered the manna daily. You remember, they could not gather sufficient on one day to do for even two days. They had to go out morning by morning and gather it. That is the only way you can nurture your spiritual life. You will have to study the Word daily. God says "day and night" (Joshua 1:8).

Perhaps you do not read the Word of God because you cannot understand it. You come across passages that are beyond your comprehension. My friend, you should read the Bible as you eat fish. Now how do I eat fish? When I come to a bone, do I take up my plate of fish and throw it away just because I have found a bone? Of course not. I pick out the bone, lay it on the side of my plate, and go on eating fish. I am not going to throw my fish away just because I find a bone. Are you going to cast God's Word aside because you come across a passage that you cannot understand? Of course not. Just leave it and go on reading the Word. Lay it aside for the time and continue your study. Keep eating fish. Keep reading the Word.

I read the Word of God as I read a letter. When I get a letter I do not turn to the first page and read a paragraph and then put it away in the pigeon-hole and a week later take it down and read a statement from the third page and then put it back in the pigeon-hole, only to take it out a few days later and look at the signature to see who wrote it. Most certainly not. When I read a letter I start at the beginning, and I read through to the end. Thus I know the contents of the letter. There is no other way to read the Word of God. I appreciate the various booklets that men have compiled, such as the *Daily Light* and others, and I use them. But I would not dream of allowing the *Daily Light* or any other book that man has compiled to take the place of the Bible. If you do that, you will never know the contents of the Book. You must read the Book itself.

I start with the first word of Genesis and I read two or three chapters a day until I have read through to the last word of Revelation. Then the next day I go back to the first word of Genesis and again I read through to the last word of Revelation. How often I have read it I do not know. I have never kept count. But I do know that I have gone through it again and again, reading the entire book from beginning to end. Thus I know something of the contents of the Book. If you really want to know it, you will have to read it like that. You will have to go through it from start to finish. Then you will become familiar with it. Read it, I say, as you would read a letter.

Prayer.

When you read God's Word, God talks to you. When you pray you talk to Him. Hence, after I have spent some time with the Book I turn to prayer, and thus I observe the Morning Watch. Now this is my authority for prayer in connection with the Morning Watch: "My voice shalt Thou hear in the morning, O Lord; in the morning will I direct my prayer unto Thee, and will look up" (Ps. 5:3).

Now there are three hindrances to the prayer life, three enemies with which we have to cope. Of course, if you merely fall down at your bedside in the morning and mumble off a few words of prayer, and then get up and hurry to your work, you will not know what I am talking about. Or if you come home at night, mumble off a few words of prayer and then fall into bed, again you will not know what I mean. I am talking about prayer, real prayer, intercessory prayer, prayer that achieves its objective. I say there are three hindrances.

(1) *Interruptions.*

Have you ever had the telephone ring when you have been at prayer? Or has the baby cried? Have friends called upon you? Have you been interrupted in one way or another? Satan knows exactly when to send the interruptions. If he can interrupt you when you are at prayer he will have wrecked the efficiency of your prayer ministry.

Now how did I get rid of interruptions? I discovered that I had to have a *time* for prayer and a *place* for prayer. As I have already stated, when I am at home I make my study the place for prayer, and I make the first hour of the morning directly after breakfast the time for prayer. Everyone knows when I am at prayer therefore interruptions are avoided. You, too, will have to have a place for prayer and a time for prayer. When I am crossing the ocean I find the most secluded part of the deck I can find, and that becomes my place for prayer. When I am at a summer conference I go out into the woods, and there, under the trees, I find a place for prayer. I go back to the same place morning by morning.

May I say that your place for prayer will become so sacred that you will think of it as holy ground. I have stained the walls of my study with the breath of my prayers. I always go back to the same place when I pray, and there God meets me. Have you a time for prayer? You may not choose the morning. Perhaps some other hour of the day will be more convenient for you. As for me, I have chosen the morning, and I find that if I observe the Morning Watch by having a place and time for prayer I can avoid interruptions.

(2) *Drowsiness.*

Have you ever become drowsy when you have been at prayer? You know what I mean. You kneel down and place your head on your arms, close your eyes and attempt to pray. Before very long you become drowsy, and at times you fall asleep. Thus drowsiness hinders your prayer life. Your body is tired and weary. You have become exhausted and you just cannot keep awake.

How did I overcome drowsiness? Let me tell you. I never kneel when I pray. I never stand or sit. I mean, of course, when I am alone, when I am observing the Morning Watch. What do I do, then? I always walk when I pray. I clear the furniture from the centre of the room and then I pace back and forth as I talk to God. I have walked hundreds of miles down through the years as I have prayed. I started doing it at the very beginning of my Christian life and I received so much blessing from it that I have continued it ever since. I find that the very best exercise that one can take is that of walking. Hence, as I walk and pray, I get all the exercise that I need.

Thus I never become drowsy. If I were to fall asleep for a single moment I would crash to the floor and would be wide awake instantly. But that has never happened. As I walk back and forth I am always wide awake. I am on the alert. I am able to pray intelligently, and I never fall asleep. You, too, can overcome drowsiness if you will walk.

(3) *Wandering Thoughts.*

You know what I mean. Just when you are concentrating on prayer you find yourself thinking, planning, arranging about the future. Thus Satan fills your mind with wandering thoughts, and instead of praying you are thinking. Well now, how are you going to get rid of wandering thoughts?

I always pray out loud. As I walk back and forth, I put my petitions into words and by praying out loud I avoid wandering thoughts. You see, I have to concentrate upon what I am saying to God just as I concentrate when I am preaching. I have no wandering thoughts when I am in the pulpit. I have to be on the alert. If you will pray out loud, you, too, will find that there will be no wandering thoughts. You, too, will be able to concentrate, and as you put your petitions into words you will be able to pray intelligently by praying out loud.

When you kneel to pray and pray quietly to yourself and to God the time seems long. Perhaps when you open your eyes you will discover that you have only been praying for five or ten minutes. That has been my experience. But when you walk and pray out loud you will discover that the time will go by so fast that you will be amazed. You will open your eyes and look at the clock, and you will discover that you have been praying for half an hour, three quarters of an hour, or perhaps an entire hour. How long do I pray? I pray until I have prayed through. I pray until I have dealt with all my problems, until I have heard from God. Thus prayer becomes an unspeakable delight.

These, then, are the three hindrances to prayer: interruptions, drowsiness, wandering thoughts. Have you overcome them and are you a prayer warrior for God? If not, you can be if you will follow my suggestions.

Thus I observe the Morning Watch. If you have never done it, then I would suggest that you start today, and that you never again let a day go by without meeting God.

There is no thrill like it. "My voice shalt Thou hear in the morning, O Lord, in the morning will I direct my prayer unto Thee, and will look up."

13

How to Live for God

Have you accepted Jesus Christ as your Saviour? Are your sins forgiven? Does God's Spirit bear witness with your spirit that you have passed from death unto life? (Rom. 8:16). Have you been born again and do you really want to live for God? If so, there are five things I would ask you to do:

First—Be sure of your salvation.

How can you know you are saved? By God's Word. The Blood makes you safe and the Word makes you sure. "These things have I written unto you that ye may KNOW that ye have Eternal Life" (1 John 5:13). Not "that ye may hope or guess or think," but "that ye may K-N-O-W—know."

It doesn't say, "These happy feelings have I given you," but, "These things have I written." Now what is written? This: "Him that cometh to Me I will in no wise cast out" (John 6:37). Have you come? Then where are you, out or in? He says He won't cast you out. Then He must have taken you in. Again it is written, "As many as received Him to them gave He power to become the sons of God" (John 1:12). Did you receive Him? Then what are you? His child, are you not?

You see, it depends on God's Word. Your feelings will change every day. Today you may "feel" saved; tomorrow, lost. But don't go by your feelings. Go by His Word. Believe what God says. Believe what is written. God's Word never changes, "Faith cometh by hearing and hearing by the Word of God" (Rom. 10:17). It is when you dare to believe, that the Spirit bears witness with your spirit that you are God's child. Thus you are assured of your salvation.

Second—Take a public stand for Christ.

I say, a public stand. Don't try to be a secret believer for it won't work. Unfurl your flag and come out into the open. Confess Christ at every opportunity. Tell others about Him. Don't hide your light. "Whosoever therefore shall be ashamed of Me and of My words of him also shall the Son of Man be ashamed" (Mark 8:38). If you want Him to acknowledge you, then you must acknowledge Him. If you want to grow rapidly, confess Him openly. Do it at once. Don't wait. Start now.

Third—Turn from all you know to be wrong.

As His Spirit indwells, you will be delivered from your sins. "Greater is He that is in you, than he that is in the world" (1 John 4:4). "If any man be in Christ, he is a new creature: old things are passed away; behold, all things are become new" (2 Cor. 5:17). He gives you a new nature, a nature that loves righteousness and hates iniquity. The Holy Spirit is His Enablement. He sets you free. You can now overcome. "Sin shall not have dominion over you" (Rom. 6:14).

But you must choose righteousness and forsake sin. Turn

your back on it. Put it away. Set your regenerated will
against it. "Abhor that which is evil; cleave to that which
is good" (Rom. 12:9). That besetting sin of yours—run
from it. Slay utterly every Canaanite alive. Destroy your
Achan. Have no dealings with sin. "If I regard iniquity in
my heart the Lord will not hear me" (Ps. 66:18). When
you mean business, God will deliver you. All you have
to do is to plead the merits of the blood and the power
of the name of Jesus. "Let not sin therefore reign in your
mortal body" (Rom. 6:12). Come clean. Be through with
sin. "Yield not to temptation." "Cease to do evil, learn to
do well" (Isa. 1:16-17).

Fourth—Spend much time in Bible study and prayer.

The more you read the Bible the more you will want to
read it. If you want to grow in grace, meet God every day.
Have a place and time for prayer and Bible study. Be a Bible Christian. Never let a day pass without spending time
alone with God. "As newborn babes, desire the sincere
milk of the Word, that ye may grow thereby" (1 Pet. 2:2).
"Where-withal shall a young man cleanse his way? By
taking heed thereto according to Thy Word" (Ps. 119:9). If
you neglect the Word you will backslide. If you learn how
to pray, you will make rapid strides in the Christian life.

Fifth—Keep busy in the service of God.

Satan always finds mischief for idle hands to do. Therefore, find something to do. Give out gospel tracts. Get
into some live, soul-winning church. Don't wait to be
asked to do something. Pray about it and get busy. Sing
in the choir. Help in the young people's work. Attend the
prayer meeting. Become a personal worker. Teach a Sun-

day School class. Go to the street meetings. Visit the poor, the sick, the imprisoned. Give your testimony. Put first things first.

Do something, but avoid cold, formal, modernistic churches. Go where the Gospel is preached and the invitation given. Associate with spiritual people, people with a testimony, people who can pray, people who love to sing gospel hymns. Keep away from choirs that only sing anthems, and ministers who never invite sinners to come down the aisles to the enquiry room.

Have nothing to do with worldly churches where the play room takes the place of the prayer room, and there is no separation. Go where people are being converted and where the message is "Ye must be born again." Never mind the denomination. If you can find a spiritual, soul-winning, missionary ministry, that is what you want.

That is all, my friend; I need say no more. If you are sure of your salvation, if you take a public stand for Christ, if you turn from all you know to be wrong, if you spend much time in Bible study and prayer, and if you keep busy in the service of God, you will do well. You will be a bright and happy Christian; God will use you in His service, and you will be a blessing wherever you go.

14

What Happens when a Christian Sins?

What happens when a Christian sins? Is he lost and lost forever? Does God cast him out, or is he still God's Child? If so, how does God deal with him? There are six things that I want to say in answering this question:

1. *The Christian does not practise sin.*
 He practises righteousness. He lives a righteous life. In 1 John 3:6, 8 and 9, we find these words: "Whosoever abideth in Him sinneth not: whosoever sinneth hath not seen Him, neither known Him... He that committeth sin is of the devil... Whosoever is born of God doth not commit sin; for His seed remaineth in him: and he cannot sin because he is born of God. In this the children of God are manifest, and the children of the devil."

The words in these verses are in the present progressive tense. The words used are "sinneth not" or "committeth sin." The child of God does not practise sin. He does not live in sin. He does not continue to indulge in sin. The practice of sin does not characterize his life. In other words, he does not keep sinning. If he does, then it is evident that he is not born of God. He still belongs to Satan.

2. *But he may fall into sin*.

"My little children, these things write I unto you, that ye sin not. And if any man sin, we have an Advocate with the Father, Jesus Christ the righteous: And He is the propitiation for our sins" (1 John 2:1-2). It is clear, then, that the Christian does not have to sin. It is not necessary for him to commit known or deliberate sin. He can be set free from sin and he need not fall into sin. "These things write I unto you, that ye sin not."

On the other hand, provision is made for the Christian who does sin. God says: "If any man sin," clearly indicating that a Christian *may* sin. He may fall into sin, even though it is not his normal life. He is like the needle of a compass. The needle always points to the north, but it is possible for some-thing to detract it and, for a moment, it may point in another direction, but inevitably it will swing back and point again north. So it is with the Christian. He does not practise sin. On the other hand, he may fall into sin. If he does, he has an Advocate, the Lord Jesus Christ. He becomes a mercy-seat, a propitiation. His sin can be forgiven.

It is like the sheep and the sow. Here is a mud puddle, for instance. The sheep gets too near and suddenly falls in. The sow does not have to fall in. The moment it sees the mud puddle it makes a bee-line straight for it and wades in of its own free will. But now what happens? The sheep immediately scrambles out, and, when it gets out, it gets as far away from the mud puddle as possible. It does not remain in the mire. The sow, on the other hand, stays in the mud puddle. It makes no effort to get out. It is now in its natural environment. It loves the mire.

So it is with the believer. He is like the sheep. He may fall in unexpectedly, but he immediately scrambles out. He confesses his sin and turns back to God. He wants to be cleansed in the precious blood. When he gets out, he immediately gets away from the mud puddle. The sheep acts like that because it is a sheep.

The unsaved man, like the sow, wallows in the mire. He loves it. It is his natural element. He seeks it and settles down in it. He stays in the mire of sin. The sow stays in the mire because it is a sow. That is its nature. So it is with the sinner. Thus you can tell a sheep from a sow, and thus you can tell God's child from Satan's child. Both may fall in, but only one stays in. The Christian does not practise sin. He does not remain in the mud puddle. The sow does, and so does the sinner. It is not because you "fall in" that you are proved an unbeliever. It is because you stay in. Both may fall in, but only one stays in. The sinner practises sin. He lives in sin. He delights in sin. The Christian, on the other hand, detests his sin and turns from it, even though in his weakness he may yield to it.

3. *If he sins God will not disinherit him and cast him out.*

He says in John 6:37: "Him that cometh to me I will in no wise cast out." God will never disinherit him. He will deal with him as with a son. Now, how does a father deal with a son? Well, let us see what God has to say about it. Suppose we turn to Psalm 89 and read from verse 30 to verse 34: "If his children forsake my law, and walk not in my judgments; if they break my statutes, and keep not my commandments; then will I visit their transgression with the rod, and their iniquity with stripes. Nevertheless my loving-kindness will I not utterly take from him, nor suffer my faithfulness to fail. My covenant will I not break, nor alter the thing that is gone out of my lips."

What will God do if His children forsake His law and walk not in His judgments? Will He break His covenant with them? Will He alter the thing that has gone out of His lips? By no means. God says He will chastise them. He will punish them. He will visit their transgression with the rod and their iniquity with stripes. He will never take His loving kindness away from them. His faithfulness will never fail. But He will judge them just as a father judges his children.

What does a father do when his children disobey? He chastises them, does he not? They have to bear their punishment, and the punishment is for the purpose of correction. He wants to win them back, and so he applies the rod. God will do the same. The punishment may be severe, very severe. When God chastises, there is suffering. But just as a father chastises and punishes, just as a father gives a thrashing when needed, so God will chastise His children. No father would show his son the door and tell him to get out and never come back. He is still his child. He is still in the family. Therefore, he corrects him by means of chastisement. God does the same.

You have the same truth set forth in 2 Samuel 7:13-15: "I will be his father, and he shall be my son. If he commit iniquity, I will chasten him with the rod of men, and with the stripes of the children of men: but my mercy shall not depart away from him."

Thus, you see, God is our Father and we are His children. When we commit iniquity He chastises us. He uses the rod. We have to bear the stripes. But, while He punishes us, He does not take away His mercy from us. We are still His children. We are still in the family, and He deals with us as members of His family.

4. *Fellowship has been broken, but confession restores it.*

Now, in 1 John 1:9, we read these words: "If we confess our sins, He is faithful and just to forgive us our sins, and to cleanse us from all unrighteousness." The moment we sin, fellowship is broken. We are no longer in communion. Sin has come between. When a child disobeys his father, he is no longer in fellowship with his father, and if he wants the fellowship restored, he must confess his disobedience and ask forgiveness. Then, and only then, is reconciliation possible.

Many of God's children, I fear, are out of fellowship with Him. They have no joy and no peace, simply because they are living in disobedience. They are not doing the things that God wants them to do. They have failed Him. They have sinned against Him. They have transgressed. He is waiting for them to confess their failure and get right so that they may be restored. As long as fellowship is broken prayer cannot be answered. Nothing but confession, restitution and forgiveness can restore it. But the moment we confess our sin He forgives us. "And the blood of Jesus Christ His Son cleanseth us from all sin" (1 John 1:7).

You see, he has got off the road. He must get back on again. The only way he can get on is by admitting his mistake and returning. If two are walking together and one wanders off, their fellowship has then been interrupted. The one who has wandered will have to come back, if the fellowship is to be renewed. That may be the reason why you are so unhappy. You are out of fellowship with God. You are His child, but communion has been interrupted. Fellowship has been broken.

5. *Thus the Christian judges himself. If he doesn't, he will be judged of God.*

Look now, if you will, at 1 Corinthians 11:27-32: "Wherefore whosoever shall eat this bread, and drink this cup of the Lord, unworthily, shall be guilty of the body and blood of the Lord. But let a man examine himself, and so let him eat of that bread, and drink of that cup. For he that eateth and drinketh unworthily, eateth and drinketh damnation to himself, not discerning the Lord's body. For this cause many are weak and sickly among you, and many sleep. For if we would judge ourselves, we should not be judged. But when we are judged, we are chastened of the Lord, that we should not be condemned with the world."

Now, to eat unworthily means to eat without having confessed the sin of which the believer has been guilty. It must be confessed and put away. There must be cleansing and forgiveness before partaking of the Communion. God tells the believer to examine himself. In other words, to judge himself. Then He says that, if he doesn't, he eats and drinks damnation to himself. However, the word is not damnation but judgment. In other words, he will be chastised.

Now that is why God says that many of His children are weak and sickly. Some, He states, have even died. I do not say that all sickness is caused by sin. Far from it. But it is possible for weakness and sickness to be the result of unconfessed sin. That may be why you have lost your job. God is dealing with you. He is judging you. You are being chastised. He wants you to be brought back into fellowship and communion once again. If He sees that you will not confess your sin, and that you are still going to dishonour Him and put Him to shame, then He may even take your life.

Now He tells us that if we will judge ourselves we shall not be judged. In other words, if we will recognize our sin and confess it and be forgiven, then God will not have to chastise us. The only way you can escape chastisement is by judging yourself. Unless you make the wrong right God will have to deal with you. If you will judge yourself, then He will not have to judge you. There is no other way to escape chastisement except by immediately confessing your sin, being forgiven, and getting right with God. If a child were to do that the father would not punish him, but if the child refuses to get right then the father has to chastise. So it is with God.

Now God says very clearly that when He judges us He chastises us. That is the nature of God's judgment. And the reason He chastises us is because we are His children and He does not want to condemn us with the world. But if we are His children, then He is going to deal with us as children. Thus we have to endure the chastisement of God. That may be why you are suffering right now. God is judging you, God is chastising you, and the only way you can get rid of God's chastisement is by confessing your sin and getting right with Him.

6. *Walking in the light procures daily cleansing.*

In 1 John 1:7 we read, "But if we walk in the light, as He is in the light, we have fellowship one with another, and the blood of Jesus Christ His Son cleanseth us from all sin." We walk in the light by obeying God, by turning from everything we know to be wrong and living in the centre of God's will. When we turn to sin we are not walking in the light, because we know that sin is wrong. Now the man who walks in the light is cleansed daily from his sin.

Jesus, you remember, wanted to wash Peter's feet. Peter refused, and Jesus told him that unless He washed his feet he could have no part with Him. Peter then wanted to be washed all over. In other words, he wanted a complete bath. But Jesus told him that if he had been washed once, if he had had a bath—in other words, if he had been converted, if he had been saved—he did not need to be washed over again. He did not need another complete bath. But his feet were being defiled as they came into contact with the dust of the road, moment by moment, and, therefore, they had to be cleansed, and so Jesus insisted on washing Peter's feet.

Now, my friend, you have been saved, you have had a complete bath, you have been born again, you are now God's child. But you are in daily contact with the world, and as long as you are—as long as you are in your body—there will be defilement, there will be stains—whether you see them or not—and you will need constant cleansing. God has made provision for you. The blood of Jesus Christ His Son continually cleanses you from all sin. That is, if you walk in the light. If you do the things that you know to be right, and abstain from the things that you know to be wrong.

May I beseech you, therefore, to turn to God the moment

you sin. You ought not to sin, but you may sin. If you do, you will repent immediately, if you are God's child, and you will ask to be forgiven. Fellowship has been broken, communion interrupted. But now, by confessing your sin and being cleansed in the blood, you are restored, and once again you are in fellowship and communion with the Lord Jesus Christ. You have now judged yourself. God will not have to judge you. If you refuse to judge yourself, then you will have to face the judgment of God. If, on the other hand, you walk in the light, the blood of Jesus Christ will cleanse you continuously from all sin.

That is what happens when a Christian sins. I am so glad that God has made ample provision, that He has recognized the possibility of sin, and that, instead of casting us out and disinheriting us when we fail Him, He deals with us as children, as members of His family. We can be forgiven and restored, and, once again, we can walk with God. Only then will His joy be ours. Only then will His peace abide in our hearts. Only then will we be in fellowship with one another and with the Lord Jesus Christ.

15

The Victorious Life

Have you accepted Jesus Christ as your Victor, and are you living a Victorious Christian Life? In 1 Corinthians 15:57 we read these words: "Thanks be to God, which giveth us the victory through our Lord Jesus Christ." Are you a Victor?

The saddest experience in the Christian life is the presence and power of sin. To be on the mountain top today and down in the valley tomorrow, to be in the eighth chapter of Romans today and back in the seventh chapter tomorrow, to be in the Promised Land today and then back in the wilderness again tomorrow, to be victorious today and defeated tomorrow—that, I say, is the saddest experience I know anything about.

God has said in unmistakable words, "Sin shall not have dominion over you." When Paul comes to the end of that terrible seventh chapter of Romans and cries out in the anguish of his soul, "O wretched man that I am! who shall deliver me?" the answer comes as though spoken by a voice from Heaven: "I thank God... Jesus Christ our Lord." So then victory is possible.

Two Classes of Sins.

Now, there are only two classes of sins known to humanity. First of all there are what we call "outward" sins, and then "inward" sins. By outward sins I mean the sins with which we are all more or less familiar, sins such as murder, drunkenness, adultery, etc. I am not talking about outward sin. If you have been saved at all, then you have already been delivered from outward sin. If not, then there is no evidence that you have ever passed from death to life.

But I am talking about inward sins. When I refer to inward sins I am referring to some sins that the average Christian does not even designate as sin at all. I am referring to such sins as worry, anxiety, unforgiveness, hatred, grudge-bearing, malice, wrath, anger, jealousy, impure thoughts—secret sins, sins that the eye of man cannot see, and a host of others that are continually rising up and clamouring for recognition. These are the sins from which the Christian must obtain deliverance.

Now, you have a besetting sin. You may overcome most of the sins to which you have been addicted, but there will be one sin that will dog your footsteps wherever you go. It is with that sin that you will have to deal. As long as you are yielding to it, God cannot use you. "If I regard iniquity in my heart, the Lord will not hear me." He will not even bend down and listen to what you say.

Sinless Perfection and Suppression.

Now I am talking about sinless perfection. I am making no reference whatever to eradication or suppression. These words are not found in the Bible, therefore I do not use them. I would a thousand times rather be wrong in my head and right in my heart, than be right in my head and wrong in my heart. I would rather have the theory wrong and the practice right, than have the theory right and the practice wrong. I want an outcome. I want to know that I am a victorious Christian.

Whenever I think of suppression I think of a story of an old Quaker woman and a new convert. They were standing side by side. Presently a terrible provocation crossed the pathway of the old Quaker woman. But during the entire time of the provocation she continued smiling just as sweetly as she had been smiling before. After it was all over the young Christian turned to her. "Say," she said, "I can't understand how you could keep your temper under a provocation such as that." The old Quaker woman, still smiling, and thinking she knew the secret of victory, turned to the younger Christian and this was her answer: "Ah, but thee didn't see the boiling inside."

My friend, if it's boiling, it's boiling. If it's there, it's there. So far as men are concerned, if you can keep it on the inside, well and good; but so far as God is concerned, you might as well explode and be through. For it doesn't matter whether you boil on the inside or the outside, if you're boiling, you're boiling. God can see it. And whether you boil on the inside or on the outside, you have lost the victory; even though you manage to hide it from the eyes of others.

I think of another story. Two boys were wrestling. One was a big boy, the other was a little boy. After a while, to the amazement of everyone, the little fellow got the big fellow down. But as soon as he got him down he got astride him and just sat there. Those standing by wondered why he did not get up and let him go. After a while a young man came along. "Say, young fellow," he said, "you've won the wrestling match, why are you sitting there? Why don't you get up and let him go?" The little fellow looked up with a grin on his face and this was his answer: "Ah," he said, "I can feel him arisin', sir." And he knew very well that if he arose, he might be underneath and the big fellow might be on top. So he thought he'd better sit tight and hold what he had, while he had what he had. "I can feel him arisin', sir." Have you ever felt him "arisin'"? Or am I talking a strange dialect that you can't understand?

You know what I mean. Just when you are having a lovely party; you have invited some Christian people to your home and you want to make a good impression. Suddenly someone steps on your toe. Someone says something behind your back. Somebody criticizes you and you are conscious of a rising inside.

You know, it is a terrible thing to have to sit on a safety-valve all your life. Safety valves have a habit of blowing off at unexpected moments. I am so glad I've found One who can take care of the safety-valve for me, while I go and do His work. My friend, Jesus Christ can deliver you from the boiling inside, from the rising within.

Dr. A. B. Simpson, the great founder of the Christian and Missionary Alliance, expressed it this way: "Everything in Jesus and Jesus Everything." That little couplet went around the world. Thousands upon thousands who had been trying to be victorious by believing a doctrine realized at last that victory was in a Person, not in a doctrine, and they stepped out of defeat into glorious blood-bought victory. Others who believed that victory was in an experience, also came to realize that victory was in a Person, and they, too, stepped out of defeat into victory.

Old Testament Examples.

Away back in the Old Testament you have it stated very clearly: "Ye shall not need to fight in this battle. Stand ye still, and see the salvation of the Lord, which He will work for you this day, for the battle is not yours, but God's." Did you ever hear of that kind of a battle? You see, God is to do the work for you. The battle is not yours, it is His. Oh, if I could get everyone to go out, saying, with each step, "The battle is not mine, the battle is the Lord's," it would spell the difference between defeat and victory.

Do you remember when Joshua went to view the walls of Jericho? He saw a man standing over against the walls and he challenged him. "Art thou for us or for our adversaries?" What did the man say? "Nay," he said, "but as captain of the Lord's host am I now come." What did Joshua say? Did he say, "Well, Captain, I'm glad to see you, but I don't need your help. I have a great army. Jericho is a very small city. We can capture it without your assistance"? Had he said that, Jericho might never have fallen. What did he say? "What saith my Lord unto his servant?" Do you remember what happened? The Lord's host, those mighty, invisible angels of God, were placed on the battlements of the walls and, with one mighty shove, they were overthrown.

My friends, the Captain of the Lord's hosts is here right now. He is saying, "You have failed. That besetting sin of yours has overcome you. Now let Me undertake for you. Let Me fight your battle. Let Me be your Victor. I'll defeat your foe, and then I'll give you the credit for the victory." Wouldn't that be wonderful?

"I'd Send Jesus to the Door."

Here is a little girl who has recently been saved. "Little girl," asks her teacher, "where is Jesus now?" She thinks for a moment and then, as she looks up into her teacher's face, with a bright smile, she answers.

"Teacher," she says, "Jesus is in my heart."

"Yes," says the teacher, "Jesus is in your heart. Now, little girl, what will you do tomorrow if Satan comes and knocks at the door of your heart?" Again she thinks. Finally she gives an answer that very few mature Christians would think of giving.

"Teacher," she says, "I'd send Jesus to the door."

Now, my friends, suppose you fail to grasp the secret of victory. Tomorrow Satan comes and knocks at the door of your heart. It is your old temptation, your besetting sin. Quickly you hurry to the door. Satan stoops down and looks through the key-hole and, as he sees you coming, he grins to himself. Many a time he has conquered you in the past and he knows he can conquer you again. You do not throw the door wide open. No-one ever sins like that. You just open it a little way, so that you can talk to Satan through the crack. You turn your temptation over as a sweet morsel. You meditate on it. Presently, before you realize what has happened, he puts his foot in the crack. Then, edging around and around, at last he is on the inside, and, once again, you have gone down in defeat.

Now, suppose you do grasp the secret of victory. Again Satan comes and knocks at the door of your heart. "Jesus! Jesus!" you exclaim.

"Yes, my child, what is it?"

"Jesus, that's Satan, that's my old besetting sin."

"Yes, my child, I know," answers Jesus. "What do you want Me to do?"

"Jesus, will You go to the door? Will You answer Satan?"

"Yes, my child, you just sit here and trust Me. I'll go and deal with your adversary."

Jesus goes to the door. Again Satan stoops down and looks through the key-hole. This time he sees, coming toward him, the Son of God. He knows that Jesus has often defeated him before and that He can defeat him again. Jesus throws the door wide open and steps out on the porch. I doubt if He will see Satan for dust down the street. Quietly He returns. "My child," He says, "you have won the victory."

"*I* have won the victory, Lord? What do you mean? *You* have won the victory."

"No, my child, you have won the victory."

"But, Lord, I have not done anything. I have just been sitting here trusting You. *You've* won the victory."

"Yes, my child. That is the way you and I are going to fight your battles in the days to come. You are going to sit still and trust. I am going to go out and do the fighting. Then I'll come back and give you the credit."

My friends, isn't that a glorious way to fight? Isn't it wonderful to have someone else to do your fighting for you? You know, you do not get hurt when someone else fights your battles. I was delicate when I was a boy. I was not big and robust and strong, like I am now. I never could do my own fighting. Whenever I had a fight on my hands I always had to go and find a bigger boy and ask him to do my fighting for me. Then all I had to do was to stand still and watch. I was never defeated. I never got hurt. I always won the victory. That, I say, is a wonderful way to fight. But so few of us are willing to fight like that. Most of us want to do our own fighting. We are not ready to let someone else do our fighting for us.

Paul Rader.

Many of you know, or have heard about, the great American evangelist, Paul Rader. I knew him very, very well indeed. Many a time he called me on the telephone and asked me to go to Chicago to preach in his great tabernacle, when he was going to be away holding a campaign somewhere. Time after time I have faced his audience of some three thousand people and I have seen the altar full, as men and women responded to the invitation. Many times I invited him to Toronto to preach for me.

But not only was Paul Rader a great evangelist, he was also a great pugilist. As a matter of fact he fought thirty-three battles in the ring and was never once knocked out.

One day I was spending an evening with him, when my curiosity got the better of me. "Mr. Rader," I said, "will you let me feel your muscle?" He looked at me somewhat perplexed and then, standing to his feet, he took off his coat, rolled up his sleeve, folded his arm and, turning to me, said: "Put it there." I felt those great steel muscles of his, and, even as I talk about it now, I can still feel them.

Now, suppose he had said to me: "My friend, I want to challenge you to a fight in the ring." Suppose I had answered, "All right, Mr. Rader, I'll be very glad to take you on." But, even while saying it, I would know perfectly well he would never have to strike me. He would just pat me gently and I would lie down, unconscious. He would just tap me a little bit and I would see stars. Nevertheless, I accept his challenge.

Immediately I find my way to Jack Dempsey, former heavyweight champion. "Mr. Dempsey," I say, "I have a fight on my hands, a fight with Paul Rader, the man who has never been knocked out, and who may some day become the heavyweight champion of the world. Would you be willing to take this fight off my hands? Would you be willing to take my name and meet Paul Rader on my behalf?" Mr. Dempsey answers, "Why, certainly. I'd be delighted to take the fight off your hands."

Well, the great night of the fight comes. I take my seat somewhere outside the ropes in an easy chair. I never have been at one of those affairs and I never expect to be, but I know I would be outside the ropes. Presently I see the huge form of Mr. Rader coming through the curtains in the farther corner, and, as I look at his great steel muscles, I am very glad that I am not inside the ropes. Then I look in the other direction and I see Mr. Dempsey coming out. Of course no-one there knows that the other man is Mr. Dempsey. Everyone thinks that Paul Rader's opponent is Oswald J. Smith. The referee gives his instructions and the fight starts.

Suddenly, to the amazement of everyone, Mr. Dempsey strikes the decisive blow and, for the first time in his life, Paul Rader goes down and is counted out. Then the referee lifts the arm of the other and calls out to the gathered thousands, "Oswald J. Smith has won." Then newspaper headlines all over the world, and, in the American papers, headlines nearly a foot deep, appear with the announcement, "New Heavyweight Champion—Oswald J. Smith,

Future Heavyweight Champion of the World!"

Listen, my friend, I would be a fool to go into the ring with Paul Rader, for I wouldn't stand a chance. But you are a greater fool when you go into the ring with Satan, for you haven't a ghost of a chance. Satan has been on the job for over six thousand years. He knows your weakest point. He knows exactly how to defeat you, and yet you think you can match him.

What should you do? You should do exactly what I would do, if Paul Rader were to challenge me. You should go and find someone bigger and stronger. And the only One I know, who is stronger than Satan, is the Lord Jesus Christ. When you are challenged you should go to Him and ask Him to fight for you. He can defeat Satan. You can be victorious as He fights your battles.

Can Such a Life be Lived?

Can such a life be lived? Let me put it this way: Has Jesus Christ ever kept you in victory for a minute? You say He has. Well, then, if He can keep you victorious for a minute, why not for a day, a month, or a year? It takes just the same current to drive the street-car one mile as it does to drive it ten miles. You are not a storage battery. God does not wind you up and leave you to yourself. You are in contact with a live wire.

As long as Peter kept his eyes on Jesus, he walked on the water. As soon as he got his eyes off Jesus, he commenced to sink. When he got his eyes back on Jesus again, he walked once more. As long as the iron is in the fire, the fire is in the iron. As soon as you take the iron out of the fire, the fire comes out of the iron. As long as you are in contact with Jesus Christ, you are victorious.

Major Whittle one time read that hymn: "I Need Thee Every Hour." "That will never do," he said. "I need Him every moment." Right there and then he sat down and wrote "Moment by moment I'm kept in His love." Only as you keep in touch with the Lord Jesus, moment by moment, will you be a victorious Christian. There is no experience that you can get at an altar that will last you for a lifetime.

How to Do It.

I want you, now, to get alone with God, to go over all your sins of the past, to make a full and complete confession, because He says that "If we confess our sins, He is faithful and just to forgive us our sins." Sin confessed is sin forgiven. Sin forgiven is sin cleansed. "The blood of Jesus Christ His Son cleanseth us from all sin" (1 John 1:7).

Then, after there has been a full and complete confession, after you have been cleansed and forgiven, then dare to take Jesus Christ as your Victor. Years ago you took Him as your Saviour. You must now open your heart and receive Him as your Victor.

Not only did the children of Israel cross the Red Sea; they also crossed the Jordan River. You may have crossed the Red Sea. You may have been converted, but have you crossed the Jordan River? Have you accepted Jesus Christ as your Victor? You may grow in grace, but there must be a starting point. You get nothing until you start. There is a beginning to everything. There must be a beginning to victory. There must be a moment when you step out of defeat into victory, when you leave the Wilderness for the Promised Land.

What If You Fail?

Now let me say something very, very important. You will go out expecting to live a Victorious Life, but you will fail again, and then you will be discouraged and you will say: "It doesn't work. I cannot be victorious."

My friend, listen. Did you ever see a little baby learning to walk? I have. What happens? Well, the baby tumbles. Then what? Does it lie down on the floor on its back and say, "Well, it's no use. I see other people walking but I'll never be able to walk"? No, never. It has a good cry. Then it immediately gets up and starts to walk again. It may have another tumble. Perhaps half a dozen. But, finally, it will find itself walking.

Now, why did it tumble? Why did it fall? Because its little legs were weak. They had to become strong. So it is with you, my friend. Your spiritual legs are weak. You haven't walked in victory for years. Don't be surprised, then, if you have a few tumbles at the beginning. Don't get discouraged. You have claimed Jesus as your Victor. Now praise Him and tell Him that He is still your Victor. Confess your failure to God. Ask Him to forgive you. Tell Him you want to be victorious. Then start again.

What will happen? Presently, to your amazement, you will discover that you are not having any more falls. You are now a victorious Christian because Jesus is living His life within.

You Cannot Live the Victorious Life.

Remember, you have never lived the Victorious Life and you never can live the Victorious Life. The only One who has is the Lord Jesus Christ. What, then, is the Victorious Life? The Victorious Life is the out-living of the indwelling Christ. As He indwells in the power of the Holy Spirit, He lives out His life from within. People see the Victorious Life being lived. You know you are not living it. You realize that Jesus Christ is living it in you and through you. You cannot live it, but He can. So you just let go and let God. That is the Victorious Life.

I've seen thousands upon thousands of orange trees. Never yet have I heard an orange tree say, "I am so afraid I may bear crab-apples instead of oranges." It just automatically produces oranges. It never once makes a mistake and produces crab-apples. Why? Because in its branches is the juice of the orange. What is in comes out. The sap within reproduces itself in the form of oranges. So it is with you. If Jesus Christ indwells in His glorious fullness, the result will be a Victorious Life.

"Thanks be unto God which giveth us the victory." How? Through our efforts, our struggles, our endeavours? No.

"Through the Lord Jesus Christ." Victory through Another. Victory through Christ. It is a gift. You cannot earn it. You cannot merit it. He gives it. It is not through your efforts. It is through Him. If you want to be a victorious Christian, you will have to receive Him as your Victor, let Him indwell you, keep in constant contact with Him by prayer and Bible study, and then, as you walk with Him, He will manifest Himself through you. That will be the Victorious Life.

Do you not want it? Well, then, confess your failures, and take Christ as your Victor. Then let Him live His own glorious, Victorious Life in and through you. Will you do it? Do it and do it—NOW.

16

Worldly Wisdom or Divine Power

Paul's admonition to the Philippians, "Have no confidence in the flesh," was never more needed than now. Great and grave dangers face the Church of Jesus Christ. More and more men are depending on education and worldly wisdom instead of on God's Dynamic.

Here, for instance, is a man who wants to argue:

"Are you a Christian?" you enquire.

"Well," answers the man, "I would like to know where Cain got his wife."

"But, my friend, is your soul saved? I am interested in your soul's salvation."

"How do you think a man should be baptized?"

"I will deal with that after you accept Christ. It really makes no difference until you are saved."

"Do you believe what the Bible says about the sun standing still?"

"My friend, I believe you need Jesus and I want to urge you to accept Him now."

"But which church should a man join?"

"No church until he knows Christ. Will you receive Him?"

Thus you keep him to the point and compel him to face the issue, for the moment you commence to answer his questions he will get you into an argument. But by dealing only with the question of his soul's salvation, the Spirit of God will, sooner or later, produce conviction.

A New Convert.

I remember a story about a very young convert. He knew nothing regarding personal work, but he did know one passage of Scripture. Approaching an infidel he invited him to Christ.

"But I don't believe in Christ," said the infidel.

"Well," responded the new convert, "the Bible says, 'He that believeth not shall be damned.'"

"But I don't believe the Bible either," responded the infidel.

"That doesn't change it," answered the other, "because God declares that, 'He that believeth not shall be damned.'"

"God! Haven't I told you I don't believe in God? I tell you there is no God," exclaimed the infidel, his wrath rising.

"And again I say," quietly responded the new convert, "that 'He that believeth not shall be damned.'"

Picking up his hat, the infidel, in a fury of rage, pushed him aside, and left the building, cursing and swearing as he went. The young convert, somewhat disappointed and humiliated, offered an earnest prayer, lamenting his lack of knowledge, and asking the Spirit of God to work. And He did. The man went home and to bed, but not to sleep. Hour after hour he tossed restlessly from side to side. All his old-time arguments upon which he had prided himself he went over one by one. Yet every now and then he would hear those solemn words: "He that believeth not shall be damned." At last, unable to bear it longer, he climbed out of bed, fell on his knees and prayed, "O God, if there be a God, save me. Reveal Thy Son to me and help me to believe." And before long he was rejoicing in Christ.

The Word, you see, is quick and powerful. It is sharper than any two-edged sword. And it alone God has promised to bless and use. Not your arguments, but His Word. It, says God, shall prosper. Oh, then, preach the Word.

Education is not a necessity. Even a knowledge of the language is not essential. Interpretation can be effective. Brainerd's interpreter was a drunken Indian, yet God blessed His Word until the Indians were stung with conviction.

Paul's Ministry.

"And I, brethren, when I came to you, came not with excellency of speech or of wisdom, declaring unto you the testimony of God."

Think of it! Paul, educated, trained, talented. Yet he made no effort to be eloquent, for well he knew that oratory was powerless to produce conviction and repentance. No, nor wisdom. All his great learning he cast aside.

"For I determined not to know anything among you, save Jesus Christ, and Him crucified!" (1 Cor. 2:2). What a confession! No wonder God so mightily used him. For here was one who had "no confidence in the flesh." In other words, he hid, as it were, his great learning and became in the sight of the people an ignoramus. He determined to know—how much? A little? No, nothing. And yet—everything. One man, but He the God-Man, Christ Jesus. And then he adds: "Him crucified," a death that carried with it the deepest disgrace known. Oh, how the Cross was despised! Yet Paul determined to put it in, for He knew its power. And the Cross is the heart, the dynamite of the Gospel. Let us never forget it, for remember, there is no Gospel without a Cross. Paul knew God's dynamite and he used it, for he wanted results, and he got them. "For the preaching of the Cross is to them that perish foolishness; but unto us which are saved it is the power of God" (1 Cor. 1:18).

"And my speech and my preaching was not with enticing words of man's wisdom, but in demonstration of the Spirit and of power" (1 Cor. 2:4).

Now we have the secret. No words of worldly allurement. Nothing of the wisdom and learning of man. That is all cast aside. Reliance is entirely upon the Holy Spirit. He is the Demonstrator of what the Gospel will do.

"But the natural man receiveth not the things of the Spirit of God: for they are foolishness unto him; neither can he know them, because they are spiritually discerned."

The natural, the unregenerate man, you see, cannot intellectually understand the things of God, because they are in a realm with which he is entirely unacquainted. With the natural he is familiar and at home, but to the spiritual he is a stranger. Hence the utter uselessness of seeking to convince him by human reasoning.

"For after that in the wisdom of God the world by wisdom knew not God, it pleased God by the foolishness of preaching to save them that believe. God hath chosen the foolish things of the world to confound the wise; and God hath chosen the weak things of the world to confound the things which are mighty; and base things of the world, and things which are despised, hath God chosen, yea, and things which are not, to bring to naught things that are:

that no flesh should glory in His presence" (1 Cor. 1:21, 27–29).

Oh, how plain, how unmistakable! The world by all its accumulated wisdom, declares Paul, failed to know God. Salvation, he continues, results from something that any believer can do—preach. Note God's choice—the foolish, the weak, the base, the despised, the nothings. And with these, these who "have no confidence in the flesh," He confounds the wise, the mighty, the worldly somebodies. And so we glory in Him and in Him alone. Blessed be God!

The Gospel.

"For I am not ashamed of the Gospel of Christ: for it is the power of God unto salvation to every one that believeth" (Rom. 1:16).

The Gospel, not your wisdom, training, education, talents or gifts; the Gospel is the power, the dynamic of God. Oh, my brethren, let me appeal to you. Let not worldly wisdom blind you to the glories of the Gospel, nor deceive you as to its power.

"Go ye into all the world and preach the Gospel to every creature." Preach it to the high and to the low. Preach it to the rich and to the poor. Preach it to the old and to the young. Preach it to the learned and to the ignorant, to royalty and to peasant alike, for all are equal in God's sight. "All have sinned," therefore all need a Saviour.

"So shall my Word be that goeth forth out of My mouth, it shall not return unto Me void, but it shall accomplish that which I please, and it shall prosper in the thing whereto I sent it" (Isa. 55:11).

17

The Highest Form of Christian Service

The highest form of Christian service is intercessory prayer. I state this without fear of contradiction. And what I am going to say now is applicable to every Christian in the world, for all may have a part. You may not be able to preach, but you can pray. It is your privilege to become an intercessor if you choose to, and thus accomplish the greatest work that God has committed to man.

Turn with me if you will to Exodus 32:31, 32, and notice here the almost unparalleled prayer of Moses as he intercedes on behalf of his people: "And Moses returned unto the Lord, and said, Oh, this people have sinned a great sin, and have made them gods of gold. Yet now, if Thou wilt forgive their sin—." And here occurs a pause indicated by a dash after the word "sin" as if Moses waited to hear God's answer before saying more, "...if Thou wilt forgive their sin—" he prays. And in the pause that follows, his heart overwhelmed with grief, he listens for God's reply; but in vain he waits for an answer; there is no response. Then, with a burden that crushes him almost to death and a love that struggles up in his heart on behalf of his people, he continues his intercession: "And if not," he prays, "blot me, I pray Thee, out of Thy book which Thou hast written."

Oh, what a prayer! How marvellously this servant of God interceded for his people! What a burden rested heavy upon his heart! It is almost impossible for us to comprehend the bitter anguish of his soul as he pleaded. How deep was his love!

Did ever man pass through such an experience? And how feeble are our petitions in comparison with this great intercessor's! Moses was willing to be for ever separated from God, to have his name blotted out of the Book of Life and be eternally lost, if only his people might be saved.

But Moses does not stand alone. There is one other who passed through the same experience, felt the same burden, endured the same agony and made the same offer. That one was Paul, the mighty apostle to the Gentiles. "I say the truth in Christ," he exclaims, "I lie not, my conscience also bearing me witness in the Holy Ghost, that I have great heaviness and continual sorrow in my heart. For I could wish that I myself were accursed from Christ for my brethren, my kinsmen according to the flesh" (Rom. 9:1-3).

What a picture of the heart of Paul! We think of him as a man filled with joy, not only rejoicing himself, but bidding others to do the same. Yet here he declares that he has great heaviness and continual heart sorrow, that he is under tremendous pressure, that he carries a burden every moment of the day and night. And oh, what a burden! How it crushes him! So great is it that he declares himself willing to be accursed, eternally separated from Christ, for the sake of his kinsmen according to the flesh. In other words, Paul feels exactly the same as Moses felt. So wonderful is his love for his own people Israel, that, after counting the cost, he is willing to lose all in order that they might gain all. And the only relief he can find is in prayer, mighty, unceasing intercession for his brethren the Jews.

And now with such examples of intercession born out of a broken, burdened heart, how lamentably weak and unreal are our prayers! Would to God we too might be thus burdened for others, that we might have power with God in the ministry of intercession.

Now I want to mention some things which it is necessary to remember if we are to engage in this, the highest form of Christian service.

Standing on praying ground

First of all, it means that we must be standing on praying ground. That is to say, we must be certain that everything is right between us and God. Unless this is the case it is useless to even attempt to pray. "If I regard iniquity in my heart," declares the inspired Word, "the Lord will not hear me." That means that God will not even listen to my prayer, let alone answer it. To be standing on praying ground is to have put away every sin, to turn from anything that grieves the Holy Spirit, and to separate myself from all that is displeasing to God. And so as we think of this, the highest form of Christian service, and resolve to become intercessors, let us make sure first of all that we are standing on praying ground and that there is nothing between us and God.

The burden for others

In the second place, intercessory prayer means that we have prayed beyond ourselves, our needs and problems, and that we are in a place and position spiritually to enter into this blessed ministry with Jesus Christ, taking upon us the burden for others in a real soul-travail, and allowing the Holy Spirit to pray through us in the will of God.

Most of the prayers recorded in the Bible are for others. Moses and Paul, as we have already seen, thought only of Israel. Our Lord Himself seldom prayed for His own needs. His burden was always for the multitudes that thronged Him on every side. Intercessory prayer is prayer for others.

That means that we put ourselves alongside of the Lord Jesus Christ, seek to know the burden of His heart, find out the plan, the programme that He wants carried out, and then pray with that in mind. So often we do not think of this. The whole burden of our prayer is centred upon ourselves. It is our needs, our desires, that are uppermost in our prayers. We must get past this. We must pray until we have dealt with everything that concerns ourselves and then launch out in intercession on behalf of others. What does God want done? What is His plan for this work or that? How best can we serve the interests of the Lord Jesus Christ and glorify Him? These are the questions that must be asked. Let us therefore wait before Him until He reveals the burden of His heart, and then, putting ourselves alongside Jesus Christ, let us intercede and bring His programme to pass.

That means that we must take into account the enablement of the Holy Spirit, for He alone knows the mind of God. The life yielded to Him will be directed, guided and illuminated, so that the petitions offered will not miss the mark. He will lead us to pray along the line of God's plan and God's purpose if we will but trust Him and place ourselves entirely at His disposal. Oh, the joy of praying with Jesus Christ! That is a different thing from praying for ourselves.

The hardest kind of work

Now I want to go on and say that intercessory prayer is without doubt not only the highest form of Christian service, but also the hardest kind of work. To the person who is not an intercessor such a statement seems absurd. Prayer to most people is looked upon as an easy occupation. Difficulties are unknown. But that is because they know nothing at all of the ministry of intercession. Their prayers, for the most part, are centred upon themselves, their loved ones and their own personal interests, with an occasional petition for the perishing heathen. They spend, perchance, five to fifteen minutes in the morning and the same again at night. To set aside a special hour during the day, or to wait before God for half a night never enters their mind. Their prayer life is spasmodic. It is considered a side issue and is readily neglected if other things demand attention. Such a person is in no way affecting the kingdom of Satan. Hence prayer, so-called, is easy.

But the Christian who enters upon the ministry of intercession will pass through a very different experience. Satan will do everything in his power to hinder and obstruct.

There will be a conscious realization of his presence and opposition.

Then, too, discouragement will cross our pathway. Again and again we will feel like giving up. No wonder the Lord gave the parable of the friend at midnight. Im-

portunity is one of the greatest requisites. We pray on for
a certain time and then because the answer does not come
we grow discouraged and give up. Thus Satan uses his
most successful weapon against us and breaks down our
determination to become intercessors.

Then, when all else has failed, he will burden us with
work. Satan would rather have us work than pray any time.
Full well he knows that prayerless work will be powerless
and fruitless. Hence if he can only keep us busy so that
we do not have time to pray he will have accomplished
his purpose.

> *Away with work that hinders prayer,*
> *'Twere best to lay it down;*
> *For prayerless work, however good,*
> *Will fail to win the crown.*

Oh, my brother, let me beg of you to take stock of your
life and to make a thorough investigation and see if everything you are doing is really essential. Perhaps you are
crowding out prayer by allowing Christian activities to
take its place. I plead with you, before it is for ever too
late, to adjust your ministry, leave out the non-essentials,
and do not allow yourself to become overloaded, but see
to it that you have time to get alone with God, and you
will accomplish more in one month than you otherwise
could in a year.

"Epaphras, who is one of you, a servant of Christ, sa-
luteth you, always labouring fervently for you in prayers"
(Col. 4:12). Why such fervency? Why so much labour?
Most of us would simply make our request before God,
believe that He had answered, and think no more about

it. But not so with Epaphras. To him it was hard work. He was a real intercessor. And so Paul describes his prayer life on behalf of others not only as "labour" but "fervent labour," or, as it is in the margin, "striving." Do we know anything about that kind of ministry?

"And being in an agony He prayed more earnestly: and His sweat was as it were great drops of blood falling down to the ground" (Luke 22:44). Thus prayed the Son of God. Even to Him prayer was the most difficult work that He had to do. Oh, yes, it was a joy, for communion with God always brings joy and blessing; but then there is the enemy to meet when prayer becomes a battle. I wonder how much we know about this kind of prayer?

The inspired Word says that He was in agony, that after He had prayed for a time He began to pray "more earnestly," and that the work was so hard, the agony so great, the burden so heavy, the pressure so terrible, that the very sweat became blood as it oozed out through the pores of His skin. What intensity! How terrific the struggle! And how far we fall short in our intercessory prayer life! How little we know of the burden that rested on the Son of God.

"Likewise the Spirit also helpeth our infirmities: for we know not what we should pray for as we ought: but the Spirit Himself maketh intercession for us with groanings which cannot be uttered" (Rom. 8:26). Here we have a picture of the prayer-life of the Holy Spirit. Even He prays as Jesus prayed. Note the language used in regard to His intercession. It was with "groanings." And in order to give some idea of the intensity and suffering it is said that the groans of the Spirit are inexpressible. No language is capable of conveying an adequate conception of the fervency of the Spirit's intercessions. They are with groanings which cannot be uttered.

The most effective weapon

Intercessory prayer is the Christian's most effective weapon. Nothing can withstand its power. It will do things when all else has failed. And the marvel is that we turn to other agencies in order to accomplish what only prayer can bring to pass. God has placed this mighty weapon in our hands and He expects us to use it. How disappointed He must be when we lay it aside and substitute natural means for supernatural work.

When D. L. Moody first visited Edinburgh, Scotland, it was literally true that within a few days the entire city was stirred to its depths. Not only so, but the whole of Scotland was more or less aroused. It was not long until the trains were bringing people into the city to attend the meetings from every part of the country, so tremendous was the interest.

What had happened? Why, God in answer to volumes of intercessory prayer that for months past had been ascending daily, had suddenly put a great concern upon the people. Thousands became anxious about their spiritual condition, and multitudes were swept into the Kingdom. It was one of the greatest, if not the greatest, outpourings of the Spirit that Scotland has ever seen or known. And now what is the result? Was it a true outcome?

I was over in the Old Country a few months ago, and this is what I discovered. The great outstanding leaders in evangelical and evangelistic work all over the British

Isles, the men and women who have accomplished the biggest things for God's Kingdom, in the large majority of cases, were converted under the ministry of D. L. Moody. Scotland has never forgotten that remarkable visitation. The secret, as everyone will admit, was first and foremost, intercessory prayer.

"The effectual fervent prayer of a righteous man availeth much" (Jas. 5:16). Such is God's estimate of intercessory prayer. The illustration that follows is taken from the ministry of Elijah. How marvellously he made use of the God-appointed method! I think of Elijah as walking around with the key of heaven in his pocket. Taking it out, he places it in the lock of the clouds, turns it, and lo, the heavens are shut and closed, so that no rain can possibly fall. Three and a half years later he takes the key again from his pocket, puts it in the same lock, turns it, and lo, the rain falls in torrents. Thus he wielded the mighty weapon of intercession and brought things to pass.

"Peter therefore was kept in prison: but prayer was made without ceasing of the church unto God for him" (Acts 12:5). Yes, Peter was kept in prison, that was man's power. Then follow two words that bring us immediately into a higher realm where mightier forces are at work—"But prayer." Thank God, the Early Church knew the power of intercessory prayer. Peter was released. God had sent His angel in answer to the cry of the Church.

Why have we turned away from it? How is it that the Church of today has such little confidence in the efficacy of intercession? What a loss is ours! Oh, that God might talk loudly to us and call us back to the days of the Early Church, until once again we are brought to realize the effectiveness of this mighty weapon, so that we, too, may bring things to pass and do a supernatural work through intercessory prayer.

The high-water mark

Intercessory prayer is the high-water mark of spiritual experience. There are many who boast of wonderful supernatural manifestations who are not intercessors. It is possible to have some of the gifts of the Spirit, and yet not to be an intercessor. To fail here is to fail everywhere, but to thus enter into fellowship with Christ is the greatest of all blessings.

You can never get higher than the throne-life. When Jesus Christ returned to the right hand of His Father it was to engage in the great ministry of intercession on behalf of His Church. For nineteen hundred years now He has been occupied in this way. In His estimation at least it is the most important work that He has to do. The throne-life is the high-water mark. To engage in this same ministry is to do down here what Christ is doing up there. The Bible says, "He ever liveth to make intercession for them" (Heb. 7:25).

My friend, you may be seeking some special gift. You may be looking for some unusual manifestation. It may be that some great emotional experience is your delight, and possibly you look down upon others who have not as yet received what you have received and consider that you are far above them in Christian experience. Let me assure you that such is not the case. The highest form of Christian service is intercessory prayer. The high-water mark of spiritual experiences an intercessory life. Unless you have attained to this you fall far short. I care not how emphatically you may boast of your spiritual experiences and of the special gifts that you have received, your ministry is void of power, your gifts valueless, if you know not how to intercede on behalf of others. The throne-life is what really counts with God.

Forgive me if I seem to speak strongly on this point. But we are living in a day when Satan has substituted everything else in the world for spirituality in the place of intercessory prayer. We need to be warned and placed on our guard lest we be deceived by his devices and miss after all the high-water mark of spiritual experience.

God's mighty instrument

Intercessory prayer is God's mighty instrument for the salvation of souls. I give here as an example the remarkable conversion of J. Hudson Taylor as related in his own words. It shows how his mother's prayers prevailed on his behalf. With gifts and talents she was not especially endowed, but she knew God, and she knew the ministry that is carried on behind the closed door. The incident reads as follows:

"Little did I know at the time what was going on in the heart of my dear mother, seventy or eighty miles away. She rose from the dinner table that afternoon with an intense yearning for the conversion of her boy, and feeling that—absent from home, and having more leisure than she could otherwise secure—a special opportunity was afforded her of pleading with God on my behalf, she went to her room and turned the key in the door, resolved not to leave that spot until her prayers were answered. Hour after hour that dear mother pled for me, until at length she could pray no longer, but was constrained to praise God for that which His Spirit taught her had already been accomplished, the conversion of her only son.

"When our dear mother came home a fortnight later, I was the first to meet her at the door, and to tell her I had such glad news to give. I can almost feel that dear mother's arms around my neck, as she pressed me to her bosom, and said, 'I know, my boy; I have been rejoicing for a fortnight in the glad tidings you have to tell me.'"

Oh, my friends, may God stir our hearts! How great is our responsibility! How wonderful are our resources! Souls are perishing on every side. Many of our relatives and loved ones are still outside the fold. We have talked to them and urged them to accept Christ, but all in vain. Year after year has gone by and they are not yet saved. Oh, that we might take upon us the burden of their souls and give God no rest until He answers and they are converted. If we truly realize the mighty instrument that God has placed in our hands we will surely wield it until results are obtained. All else may fail, but intercessory prayer is bound to avail. God cannot deny Himself.

God's all powerful agency

Intercessory prayer is God's all powerful agency for the outpouring of the Spirit. No revival has ever yet been given apart from this ministry. Someone has prayed. Go, if you will, to the records of the great awakenings for years past and you will find that the secret, the source, has been prayer. God has burdened a little group here and there, sometimes only two or three in number, but these have so given themselves to intercessory prayer that the result has been a mighty outpouring of the Holy Spirit.

The mystery of the great awakening under D. L. Moody in the church where he preached one Sunday night in England, when hundreds were swept into the Kingdom, for some time remained unsolved, but at last the secret came to light.

Two sisters, we were told, lived together. One was an invalid. Some years before she had picked up a newspaper and read an account of the work of the great American evangelist, D. L. Moody. A burden settled down upon her. From that day she began to pray that God would send Moody to England and that he might preach in her church. At last after praying daily her request was granted. Her sister came home one morning and told her that a man by the name of Moody had preached.

Under a great burden the invalid shut herself in and refused to be seen. All that afternoon she pled with God, with the result that showers of blessing fell upon the congregation and hundreds were saved at the close of the evening service. That was the beginning of Moody's great work in the British Isles. God had signally set to His seal and it all came about as the result of an invalid's intercession.

When I was holding a city-wide campaign in Ballymena, where I faced the largest crowds that had ever gathered, I went to the little old school house where the four young men had wrestled with God in prayer, prayer that resulted in the great Irish Revival of 1859—travailing, prevailing prayer.

Let me quote from the lectures of Charles G. Finney, the man who prayed down revivals. This incident proves again that God's all powerful agency in true revival work is intercessory prayer. It reads as follows:

"A pious man in the western part of this state was suffering from consumption. He was a poor man, and was ill for years. An unconverted merchant in the place, who had a kind heart, used to send him now and then some things for his comfort, or for his family. He felt grateful for the kindness, but could make no return, as he wanted to do. At length he determined that the best return he could make would be to pray for the man's salvation. So he began to pray, and his soul kindled, and he got hold of God. No revival was taking place there, but, by and by, to the astonishment of everybody, this merchant came right out on the Lord's side. The fire kindled all over the place, a powerful revival followed, and multitudes were converted.

"This poor man lingered, in this condition of weakness, for several years. After his death, I visited the place, and his widow put into my hands his diary. Among other entries was this: 'I am acquainted with about thirty ministers and churches.' He then went on to set apart certain hours in the day and week to pray for each of these ministers and churches, and also certain seasons for praying for different missionary stations. Then followed, under different dates, such facts as these: 'Today I have been enabled to offer what I call the prayer of faith for the outpouring of the Spirit on —— Church, and I trust in God there will soon be a revival there.' Under another date he had written: 'I have today been able to offer what I call the prayer of faith for —— Church and trust there will soon be a revival there.' Thus he had gone over a great number of churches, recording the fact that he had prayed for them in faith that a revival might soon prevail among them, and it did.

"She told me that he was so exercised in prayer during his sickness, that she often feared he would 'pray himself to death.' The revival was exceedingly great and powerful in all the region, and the fact that it was about to prevail had not been hidden from this servant of the Lord. According to His Word, 'the secret of the Lord is with them that fear Him' (Ps. 25:14). Thus this man, too feeble in body to go out of his house, was yet more useful to the world and the Church of God than all the heartless professors in the country. Standing between God and the desolations of Zion, and pouring out his heart in believing prayer, 'as a prince he had power with God and with men, and prevailed' (Gen. 32:28).

"There are two kinds of means requisite to promote a revival: the one to influence men, the other to influence God. Prayer is an essential link in the chain of causes that lead to a revival, as much so as truth is. Some have zealously used truth to convert men, and laid very little stress on prayer. They have preached, and talked, and distributed tracts with great zeal, and then wondered that they had so little success. And the reason was that they forgot to use the other branch of the means, effectual prayer. They overlooked the fact that truth, by itself, will never produce the effect, without the Spirit of God, and that the Spirit is given in answer to prayer."

Prayer and the Word

There is one passage in the Bible that has been more or less of a motto to me for years past. It is the statement found in Acts 6:4, and reads as follows: "We will give ourselves continually to prayer and to the ministry of the Word." What an ideal vocation! Everything else was considered secondary. The greatest thing that the apostles could possibly do for the Kingdom of God was to give themselves first to prayer, then to the ministry of the Word. And you will notice that prayer precedes preaching.

Oh, my brethren, let me entreat you to lay greater emphasis on this part of your work. To minister the Word apart from prayer is impossible. The two are inseparably connected. He who would preach powerfully must pray effectively. To prevail with God is to prevail with man. Therefore let us give ourselves as never before in these closing days of the Age to intercessory prayer, the highest form of Christian service.

18

"Take Heed Unto Thyself"

There are four words to which I want to call your attention. You will find them in First Timothy, the fourth chapter, and the sixteenth verse: "Take heed unto thyself." These are the words of the Apostle Paul to Timothy and they are of paramount importance: "Take heed unto thyself."

Well did one of the writers of the Old Testament say: "They made me the keeper of the vineyards; but mine own vineyard have I not kept" (Song of Sol. 1:6). Many a preacher who cares for the vineyards of others neglects his own. "Take heed unto thyself."

Water can only rise to its own level and no higher. What the preacher is, his congregation will be. Show me a spiritual pastor, and I will show you a spiritual congregation. Show me a worldly pastor, and I will show you a worldly congregation. Show me a carnal pastor, and I will show you a carnal congregation. Show me a soul-winning pastor, and I will show you a soul-winning congregation. Show me a missionary pastor, and I will show you a missionary congregation. "Like priest, like people," said one of old. How true! The people will be what the pastor is.

Suppose you send a carnal missionary to the foreign field and then go out in five years' time and examine his converts. What will you find? You will discover that they, too, are carnal. Suppose you send a spiritual missionary to the field and in five years' time go out and examine his converts. Again, what will you find? You will discover that they, too, are spiritual. "Like pastor, like people." The converts will be what the pastor is. How great, then, is the responsibility of the leader.

"That which is born of the flesh is flesh." That which is born of vegetable is vegetable. That which is born of fruit is fruit. That which is born of fish is fish. That which is born of bird is bird. That which is born of animal is animal. That which is born of man is man. In other words, you cannot cross the species. You can get new varieties, but you cannot get new species. That is why the Bible says: "That which is born of the flesh is flesh, and that which is born of the Spirit is spirit" (John 3:6).

There again you have the same truth—like pastor, like people. The flesh always remains flesh. Vegetables never become fish. Birds are never changed to animals. "That which is born of the flesh is flesh." Flesh it is, and flesh it always will be. You cannot possibly change it. If you are spiritual, your people will be spiritual. If you are carnal, your people will be carnal. If you are worldly, your people, too, will be worldly. Water, I say, can only rise to its own level, and no higher.

Herein lies a great lesson, a lesson that but few have learned. You cannot lift others to the level of your preaching, nor can you lift them to the level of your teaching. You can only lift them to the level of your own spiritual experience. They will be what you are. Hence the importance of obtaining and maintaining a deeply spiritual experience of your own. Many a pastor preaches a great sermon and then wonders why the members of his congregation do not rise to the level of his preaching. It is absolutely impossible. They will be what he is. He can lift them to the level of his experience, but he cannot lift them to the level of his preaching.

If you would produce spiritual results, you yourself must be spiritual. You may preach and teach the deepest truths, but you will discover that the lives of those to whom you speak are not being transformed by your preaching, simply because your life does not back up what you say. It is what you are that counts.

God's order is unchangeable. Your pet dog can never become your child. Dog it is, and dog it will always remain, regardless of your teaching and instruction. Fruit always produces fruit and nothing else. "That which is born of the flesh is flesh."

In other words, that which is born of carnality is carnality. That which is born of worldliness is worldliness. That which is born of spirituality is spiritual. Spirituality in you produces spirituality in others. No wonder, then, Paul said to Timothy, "Take heed unto thyself."

It is all summed up in the burning words of the immortal Bounds: "The man makes the preacher. God must make the man. The messenger is, if possible, more than the message. The preacher is more than the sermon. Preaching is not the performance of an hour. It is the outflow of a life. It takes twenty years to make the man. The true sermon is a thing of life. The sermon grows because the man grows. The sermon is forceful because the man is forceful. The sermon is holy because the man is holy. The sermon is full of the divine unction because the man is full of the divine unction. The sermon cannot rise in its life-giving forces above the man. Dead men give out dead sermons, and dead sermons kill. Everything depends on the spiritual character of the preacher."

It is so easy to become professional. The man who is preaching for a living will never succeed, but if he is preaching for what he would gladly do for nothing he has caught the vision. God's Word should be a fire burning in his bones. He should preach because he cannot do otherwise. He must see to it that he does not lose his first love and that he is always on fire. Let him take his work seriously and God will make him a blessing. "Take heed unto thyself."

19

A Birthday Prayer

On November 8th, 1927, my thirty-eighth birthday, I prayed this prayer: *"Lord, make me a man after Thine own heart."* Work faded out of sight; things that before seemed important disappeared; everything in which I was interested took a secondary place, and my own inner life before God was all that mattered, all that was really worth while. And as I paced back and forth in my study that day I prayed, and prayed in the Spirit: *"Lord, make me a man after Thine own heart."*

> *I want, dear Lord, a heart that's true and clean,*
> *A sunlit heart with not a cloud between;*
> *A heart like Thine, a heart divine,*
> *A heart as white as snow,*
> *On me, dear Lord, a heart like this bestow.*

I saw as I had never seen before, that the big thing was not the work I was doing, the books I was writing, the sermons I was preaching, the crowds that gathered, nor the success achieved; but rather the life I was living, the thoughts I was thinking, heart holiness, practical right-eousness; in a word: my transformation, by the Spirit, into Christ-likeness.

There came to me with new and deeper meaning than ever before the words: *"Oh, for a closer walk with God!"* And my heart went out in a cry of anguish for such an experience. *"That I might know Him."* Thus prayed the great Apostle. "Christ in you," he said again. And then, *"Christ liveth in me."* Yes, *"Noah walked with God";* *"Enoch walked with God."* Could not I? Am not I more precious to God than my work, my possessions? God wanted me, not merely my service.

After that He led me out in prayer, a prayer that would make me *a man after His own heart,* and these were the petitions: "Lord, here are my hands; I consecrate them to Thee. May they never touch anything that Thou wouldst not have them touch, or do anything that would dishonour Thee. And here are my feet; I dedicate them to Thee. May they never go where Thou wouldst not be seen. Here, Lord, are my eyes. May they never look upon anything that would grieve Thy Holy Spirit. May my ears never listen to anything dishonouring to Thy name. May my mouth never be opened to speak a word that I would not want Thee to hear. May my mind never retain a thought nor an imagination that would dim the sense of Thy presence. May my heart know no love, and cherish no feeling that is not of Thee. Amen!"

> *Lord, I give my all to Thee,*
> *Friends and time and earthly store,*
> *Soul and body, Thine to be,*
> *Wholly Thine forever more.*

God, I saw, demanded my *undivided attention.* Everything else must take a second place. Friends and loved ones, home, money, work—all, even though legitimate—

all must give way to Christ. Day and night my *undivided attention* must be given to Him. God first! Such must be my attitude toward Him. Only then would He be able to bless and use me. Only thus could I satisfy His heart of love. For in my relationship to God I saw that none other and naught else must ever come between. That just as a husband comes first in the affections of his wife, and vice-versa, so God must come first in my heart. And just as no marriage can ever be a happy marriage where either husband or wife withhold their *undivided attention* from each other, so my fellowship with God could only be complete when He had my undivided attention. He would have me wait on Him continually.

> *All for Jesus, all for Jesus!*
> *All my being's ransomed powers;*
> *All my thoughts, and words, and doings,*
> *All my days and all my hours.*

And what He asked of me that day He asks of all alike. Can it be that we deny Him His right? Is there anything in this world worthy of that attention He claims? Why, then, do we withhold what He asks? Is true joy to be found outside of God? Can we be happy with "things"? Do "things" satisfy? "A man's life consisteth not in the abundance of the things which he possesseth" (Luke 12:15). God has made us for Himself. He longs for our fellowship and communion. To walk with Him moment by moment, right here in the midst of a wicked and perverse generation, in a world that has no use for a separated, Holy Ghost life, a world whose God is Satan—to walk with God as the sainted Brainerd and the seraphic Fletcher walked when they were here, to live as pilgrims and strangers in a world

that crucified our Lord—that is His design and His purpose for us. How then can we bear to disappoint Him, and
thus fail to win His approbation?

God wants us to be one hundred percent for Him. And so
the question arises: Are we *out and out* for Jesus Christ?
Are we *wholly God's?* Not ninety percent, mark you, but
one hundred percent. Completely given over to God. Let
us ask Him, then, to detach us from "things"; to detach
us from the world, from our families and homes, from
all that is meant by the "flesh"; to so wean us that we can
give Him our *undivided attention*. There is much in the
flesh that is legitimate. Can we deny ourselves even that
which is legitimate for the Kingdom of Heaven's sake if
our ministry should necessitate separation from our loved
ones even for long periods at a time, in order that we may
be *wholly God's?* And can we by His grace so rise above
the world and the flesh in our detachment that we will find
Jesus Himself, through His indwelling Spirit, sufficient to
enable us to live *out and out* for Him, exclaiming from a
heart filled with praise: "Jesus satisfies"? That is what He
taught me, and that is what I mean when I talk of being
wholly God's, *out and out* for Jesus Christ, one hundred
percent for Him, and thus becoming *a man after God's
own heart*.

So, then, to be a man after God's own heart means to put
God first; to walk with Him every moment; to do nothing
that would displease Him and to allow nothing that would
grieve Him; to live a life of practical righteousness and
holiness before Him; to give Him our undivided attention,
and to love Him supremely.

David, you remember, was *a man after God's own heart*.
If David, after his failure, could be such a man, cannot I,

cannot you? "Daniel purposed in his heart that he would not defile himself" (Dan. 1:18). Let us "purpose," and God will give the enabling power.

For it is in this way that we become Christ-like; and that is God's highest ambition for us, viz., that we should be like His Son, transformed into the same image. To be a Christian for ten years and to be no more like Jesus then than at the time of conversion, is a tragedy. There are some who have only been saved six months who are more like Christ than others who have been on the way for six years. Only those who spend much time in His presence will ever become like Him. Only those who give Him their undivided attention will really come to know Him.

To get His best we must give Him our best. To become men and women after His heart we must let Him have our undivided attention. To win we must surrender. To live we must die. To receive we must give.

And, oh! the sweetness of such a life, the joy of His fellowship! There is nothing like it on earth. All the success in the world will not compensate for it. He is "the Lily of the Valley," "the Bright and Morning Star," "the Rose of Sharon," "the Chiefest among Ten Thousand," "the One Altogether Lovely." Friends can never mean so much. Even loved ones disappoint. Money brings its burdens, and fame its bitterness. But He, He satisfies. God is never a disappointment. To walk with Him is the sweetest thing on earth. To know that all is well, that there is nothing between, that no black cloud of sin hides His face—ah! that is Heaven indeed.

Then let us pray it, mean it and live it: *"Lord, make me a man after Thine own heart."*

RHP Essential Classics

T. AUSTIN-SPARKS
The School of Christ
The inner working of the Holy Spirit

E. M. BOUNDS
Power Through Prayer
A stirring exhortation to pray

JOHN BUNYAN
The Pilgrim's Progress
The classic allegory of the Christian life

CHARLES FINNEY
Revival
God's way of revival

A. P. FITT
D. L. Moody
The life of the great evangelist

ROY HESSION
The Calvary Road
The way of personal revival
Our Nearest Kinsman
The message of hope from the book of Ruth
Not I, but Christ
*The Christian's relationship with Jesus explained
from the life of David*

RHP Essential Classics

ROY HESSION (continued)
The Power of God's Grace
The way of peace, joy and genuine revival
We Would See Jesus
Seeing in Jesus everything we need
When I Saw Him
Renewing your vision of Jesus
My Calvary Road
Roy Hession tells his own story

F. & M. HOWARD TAYLOR
The Biography of James Hudson Taylor
The life of a man of God

DAVID WILKERSON
Hallowed Be Thy Names
Knowing God through His names
Hungry For More of Jesus
The way of intimacy with Christ

ANDREW MURRAY
Absolute Surrender
A call to radical, Spirit-filled Christianity
The Full Blessing of Pentecost
Power from on High
Humility
The way to victory in the Christian life

RHP Essential Classics

ANDREW MURRAY (continued)
The True Vine
Fruitfulness and stability in Jesus
Waiting on God
Allowing the power of God into our lives and ministries

OSWALD J. SMITH
The Enduement of Power
Being filled with the Holy Spirit
The Man God Uses
How anyone can be used powerfully by God
The Revival We Need
A heart-stirring cry for revival

R. A. TORREY
How to Pray
Praying with power and authority
How to Study the Bible
Profit and pleasure from the Word of God

Please ask for these titles at your local Christian bookshop

RHP Essential Classics

Not I, but Christ

by Roy Hession

This is a book of wonderful theology, that goes to the heart of our difficulties as humans and as Christians, and portrays it through the beautiful story of David's life.

"The story of the Bible can be regarded simply as the story of two men, Adam and Christ. It is the story of the sin of the first man and his failure to fulfil God's intentions, and the coming of the second Man to rescue the first from his miseries and take over from him. And the story continues right up to the present, for Adam lives today as surely as Jesus Christ does.

"The Old Testament is full of types and foreshadowings of Christ, and nowhere in its pages is the story of the first man and the second Man so clearly typified as in the history of Israel's first two kings, Saul and David. I am not concerned merely to show the beautiful parallels between David and Christ, but to see in it all a pictorial presentation of certain great truths of the New Testament with regard to the Christian life, notably of the words, 'not I, but Christ'—perhaps the most complete description in the New Testament of the heart of the Christian life and how it is to be lived." —ROY HESSION

"This is devotional writing of a very high quality."
—DAVID WINTER

Roy Hession's first book, *The Calvary Road*, has been an international best-seller, with millions of copies sold.

RHP Essential Classics

Power Through Prayer
by E. M. Bounds

E. M. Bounds has a message: We need to pray. Whereas much of the church is focussing on methods and education, Bounds says the answer to the lack of power in Christian service is simply prayer. Bounds identifies the errors that many make which lead to failure, and uses the lives of great men of God as examples to show the absolute necessity of a serious prayer life. This rousing exhortation should leave a deep impression.

"What the Church needs today is not more machinery or better, not new organizations or more and novel methods, but men whom the Holy Spirit can use—men of prayer, men mighty in prayer. The Holy Spirit does not flow through methods, but through men. He does not come on machinery, but on men. He does not anoint plans, but men—men of prayer."

—E. M. BOUNDS

EDWARD MCKENDREE BOUNDS studied law and went on to practise as an attorney for several years. During the Third Great Awakening in America, he felt the call to preach. At the age of twenty-four he was made Pastor of Missouri Methodist Church. He pastored several successful churches, but was above all known as a man of prayer, rising to pray for three hours each morning. His writings on prayer have been best-sellers ever since.

RHP Essential Classics

Waiting on God
by Andrew Murray

The importance of waiting on God cannot be over-emphasized. In a world marked by frenetic activity, Andrew Murray shows that this unspectacular work opens the door to God's power in any situation. When our instinct calls us to work, it is often more important to wait—that is, to look to God to come into the situation—and then to work in His power.

"All that the Church and its members need for the manifestation of the mighty power of God in the world is the return to our true place, the place of absolute and unceasing dependence upon God. Let us strive to see what the elements are that make up this most blessed and needful waiting upon God. It may help us to discover the reasons why this grace is so little cultivated, and to feel how infinitely desirable it is that the Church, that we ourselves, should at any price learn its blessed secret."
—ANDREW MURRAY

ANDREW MURRAY (1828–1917) was born in South Africa where he served God as a pastor and evangelist. His devotional writing brought him world-wide renown and he became much in demand as a Bible teacher and conference speaker. Author of numerous books, his other titles include *The True Vine*, *Humility*, *The Full Blessing of Pentecost* and *Absolute Surrender*.

RHP Essential Classics

Humility

by Andrew Murray

This book has been definitive in the lives of many. Andrew Murray says that humility lies at the very heart of a successful Christian life. When we came to God for salvation, it was in admitting our need that we found grace. So in every stage of our walk, it is by admitting our lack and realising our utter dependence on God that we are victorious. Moreover, in that God was willing to humble Himself, it is by walking in lowliness of mind that we bear the strongest sign that we are the children of God.

"When I look back upon my own religious experience, or round upon the Church of Christ in the world, I stand amazed at the thought of how little humility is sought after as the distinguishing feature of the discipleship of Jesus. In preaching and living, in the daily intercourse of the home and social life, in the more special fellowship with Christians, in the direction and performance of work for Christ,—alas! how much proof there is that humility is not esteemed the Cardinal virtue, the only route from which the graces can grow, the one indispensable condition of true fellowship with Jesus." —ANDREW MURRAY

ANDREW MURRAY (1828–1917) was born in South Africa where he served God as a pastor and evangelist. His devotional writing brought him world-wide renown and he became much in demand as a Bible teacher and conference speaker. Author of numerous books, his other titles include *The True Vine*, *Absolute Surrender*, *The Full Blessing of Pentecost* and *Waiting on God*.